INVESTING

Stock Trading, Investing for Beginners and Trading Forex

By Sam Sutton

~~~

© Copyright 2018 By Sam Sutton
All Rights Reserved

The transmission, duplication or reproduction of any of the following work including specific information will be considered an illegal act irrespective of if it is done electronically or in print. This extends to creating a secondary or tertiary copy of the work or a recorded copy and is only allowed with express written consent from the Publisher. All additional right reserved.

The information in the following pages is broadly considered to be a truthful and accurate account of facts and as such any inattention, use or misuse of the information in question by the reader will render any resulting actions solely under their purview. There are no scenarios in which the publisher or the original author of this work can be in any fashion deemed liable for any hardship or damages that may befall them after undertaking information described herein. This book should not be taken as financial or investment advice, and the author does not take any responsibility for inaccuracies, omissions, or errors which may be found therein.

Additionally, the information in the following pages is intended only for informational purposes and should thus be thought of as universal. As befitting its nature, it is presented without assurance regarding its prolonged validity or interim quality. Trademarks that are mentioned are done without written consent and can in no way be considered an endorsement from the trademark holder.

The contents of this book are intended to convey general information only. You should not treat any information herein as a call to make any particular decision regarding cryptocurrency usage, legal matters, investments, taxes, cryptocurrency mining, exchange usage, wallet usage, etc. It is strongly suggested that you seek advice from your own financial, investment, tax, or legal adviser. This book should not be taken as financial or investment advice, and the author does not take any responsibility for inaccuracies, omissions, or errors. The author of this work is not responsible for any loss, damage, or inconvenience caused as a result of reliance on information as published on, or linked to, this book.

The author of this book has taken careful measures to share vital information about the subject. May its readers acquire the right knowledge, wisdom, inspiration, and succeed.

TABLE OF CONTENTS

STOCK TRADING 5
Introduction 6
Chapter 1: Starting Out in the Stock Market 7
Chapter 2: Picking the Right Stock 15
Chapter 3: Hazards of the Stock Market 23
Chapter 4: Top Ten Tips for Beginners and Pros Alike 28
Chapter 5: Money Management and the Stock Market 35
Conclusion 36

INVESTING FOR BEGINNERS 37
Introduction 38
Chapter 1: Why You Should Be Growing Your Money 39
Chapter 2: How Compound Interest Works 42
Chapter 3: Things to Know Before You Invest 47
Chapter 4: Investing in Stocks 53
Chapter 5: Investing in Real Estate 57
Chapter 6: Investing in Bonds 62
Chapter 7: Investing in Business Partnerships 64
Chapter 8: Investing in Precious Metals 67

Chapter 9: Investing Strategies *69*

Conclusion *73*

TRADING FOREX 74
Introduction *75*

Chapter 1: The Basics of the Forex Market *77*

Chapter 2: Requirements to Start Trading *82*

Chapter 3: The Mechanics of Trading *86*

Chapter 4: Analytical Approach to Forex *94*

Chapter 5: Value Trader Approach to Forex *100*

Conclusion *103*

STOCK TRADING

The Beginner's Guide to Turning the Stock Market into Your Personal ATM

By Sam Sutton

~~~

INTRODUCTION

So, you want to learn a bit about the Stock Market and how to make some extra money through it. No problem. You've downloaded the right book. You can now officially check off the first item on your "to do" list -- given that item is "download the best and most comprehensive guide to the stock market for beginner's."

But all joking aside, the stock market is a dangerous game to play. Yes, it's true that trading stocks is a method with which someone may make a large amount of money, but the exact opposite is also true: There's a decent chance that someone may lose money as well. Trading stocks on the stock market is a sort of gamble at time, you'll be playing with fire. You'll be playing with fire while gambling. It's not a great combination.

But, with the tips and guidance provided in this book, you can minimize your chance at burning yourself -- or, in a more literal sense, losing money.

It won't be easy. Like all money-making ventures, working with the stock market requires practice, skill, patience, a little bit of luck, and a good amount of know-how. It's pretty difficult to write a book about "how to get luckier," so these pages are filled with tips and tricks to help you learn and practice the basics, developing the proper skills, and understanding the basic know-how associated with trading stocks.

CHAPTER 1: STARTING OUT IN THE STOCK MARKET

Chances are, if you're new at trying something-- everything from tying your shoes to performing surgery. Like everything else you could possibly do, trading stocks take practice. You won't be good right away and that's perfectly acceptable.

That being said, mistakes are to be expected, but the mistakes are with your money. You have to be cautious with how quickly you jump into the stock market ocean; too quickly and you have a high chance to lose a lot of your well-earned money, too quickly and you may lose your chance to buy the perfect stock at the perfect price.

There are tons of variables that go into buying, selling, and trading stocks that many people don't consider when they first enter into the game. Luckily, you were smart enough to download this book before diving in head first.

The first chapter covers the basics that everyone needs to know when they first enter the stock market. The sections are divided up into commonly asked questions to better help you, the reader, find the answers or information you're looking for.

First thing's first...

What are Stocks?

The companies offer up little bits of ownership (called stocks) to anyone who wants to buy them. When someone buys stocks, the company is then allowed to use that money to do with as they please (usually this money goes to products, or property, or other assets the company needs to grow).

Two basic things happen when someone invests in a company and buys stock:

1. The buyer legally owns a small portion of the company
   a. Usually, a single stock is worth very, very little of the company's overall ownership.
   b. Rather than "owning some of a company," the buyer owns stocks in said company.
2. The company or business gains money from the sale to use to improve their company.

What Exactly is the Stock Market?

The stock market is a general term used to define a place (either a physical location, or a digital server) where stocks are sold, bought, and traded. Where many first time investors get confused in the terminology involved.

For example:

- An investor is a person that buys stock in one or multiple companies.
- A stock <u>market</u> is a term used to describe anywhere that deals with stocks and the trading of stocks.
  - This term is often used when teaching individuals about trading stock at a stock exchange, but can also be used to describe the entire process of trading stocks.
- A stock <u>exchange</u>, on the other hand, is a specific location that deals in the buying, selling, and trading of companies' stocks.

To help you keep these terms straight in your head, think about when you go to get pizza for dinner. If you say "I'm going to get pizza for dinner," it allows people to know what you're doing, but doesn't tell them the details. Anyone listening in understands that you're going to get a pizza from somewhere. Saying "I'm going to get pizza for dinner" is equivalent to the stock market. It's a general statement that tells people basically what you're doing in a nutshell.

If you were to say "I'm going to Domino's to pick up a pizza," you're telling anyone that's listening what you are doing and where. Domino's Pizza is the stock exchange you choose to use.

Just remember: The <u>stock market is general</u>, the <u>stock exchange is specific</u>.

The stock market as a whole allows companies to put themselves out there to the public. This creates a sort of mutually beneficial (or mutually destructive) relationship between the company and its investors.

What is a Stock Exchange Then?

Stock exchanges are the individual places that a person may buy, sell, or trade stocks. While the term "Stock Market" refers to the business, as it were, of buying, selling, and trading stocks, the exchanges that make up the stock market are the veritable storefronts of the stock trading world.

Some stock exchanges are common in media such as film and television shows to show the hussle and bussle associated with the business world. The most commonly named stock exchange is the New York Stock Exchange (also known as NYSE or "The Big Board"). The New York Stock Exchange is the largest stock exchange in the world and more than 1.5 billion dollars can be bought, sold, and traded through the New York Stock Exchange daily. Whenever a movie shows crowds of men and women in suits yelling and waving papers around in a room full of television monitors, they are usually depicting this specific stock exchange.

While a large percentage of the larger stock exchanges (the New York Stock Exchange being a prime example) are stressful and fast-paced and a bit over the top for anyone who hasn't made a living out of trading stocks, there are alternatives for any person just wanting to dip their big toe, so to speak.

A relatively recent form of stock exchanges are the online stock exchanges, which are any held through a website or internet domain. They often times require a subscription fee to use their services, but offer a much more relaxed environment for anyone just starting out.

Are there risks involved with online stock exchanges? Of course there are. There is still that looming risk of losing money through poor decisions or plain old bad luck, but there isn't the stress and fast moving atmosphere most people associate with buying, selling, and trading stocks.

In either case (whether you prefer to go into a physical location to trade stocks, or decide to stay home and do it on the computer), there are tons upon tons of options to choose from. Each stock exchange functions the same, more or less, with a few tweaks to rules, subscriptions, and other details here and there, so if you can learn to use one, you probably will do alright with the others.

In terms of physical location stock exchanges, it depends on where you live or work. You'll have to do some research regarding the surrounding areas to see what is available to you. You can also find a <u>stockbroker</u>.

A stockbroker is someone you pay to buy and sell stocks for you. And don't worry, he or she will have your best interests at heart because, after all, the more you make, the more he or she makes in the process.

If you would rather dive into the world of online stock exchange, there are still plenty of choices to choose from, and chances are you've seen a commercial for one or two over the last few years.

Commonly used and popular online stock brokerages include:

- Scottrade
- Tradestation
- Etrade
- Ameritrade
- And others.

You'll have to look more into the details of each individual brokerage to find one that suits your needs best (never just go with the first one you happen upon, always compare).

How Does Someone Make Money Buying and Selling Stocks?

The entire purpose of buying, selling, and trading stocks is to make money. Sure, a lot of people do it as a hobby in their free time (or as a full-fledged career), but no one wants to lose money on the stock market.

With that goal in mind, there are two possible ways to make money buying, selling, and trading stocks on the stock market:

1. Buy Low Priced Stocks Then Sell Them When They Go Up in Price.

Buying and selling stocks when the price is right is a good way to gain or lose a chunk of your money in an instant. This is the strategy that introduced the idea of "buy low, sell high" which you may have heard once or twice in your lifetime.

Buying stocks with a low price point (usually companies that are just starting out, or companies that aren't doing so well) will allow you to buy more at a lower price and hold onto them until their price goes up. Once the stocks' prices have increased to an amount you're happy with, you can sell them on the exchange. Because of the rise in price, your selling them for more than you originally bought them for.

Here's a trick that many people don't consider in the long run: If you buy a lot of stocks at a low price (maybe even several hundred or thousand) and the price only goes up a few dollars, you have to remember that the price of each and every stock you bought went up. Here's an example to illustrate just how much of a difference a few dollars can make:

Let's say you purchase 500 stocks of a company at 10 dollars a piece. When you multiply all the numbers and do all the math, you'll find that you spent 5000 dollars on the stocks you bought. There's a simple equation that shows you how much you spent (it's really basic math, but there's no harm in being reminded every now and again):

Number of stocks bought + price per stock = total dollars spent

In this instance, our equation would look like this:

$$500 \times \$10.00 = \$5000$$

Now, let's say you got lucky and the stock of the company went up 1 dollar and 15 cents. It's not a huge jump in price (it's less than a price of a soda, after all). How much can that small increase in price really be worth in the long run?

$$500 \times (\$10.00 + \$1.15) = ?$$

Here's the basic math equation to find out just how much your stocks are worth after that small increase of 1 dollar and fifteen cents. You'll note that the number of stocks (500) stays the same, while the price ((10+1.15)) changes to include the increase in worth.

So, we have the equation, now we just do the math...

$$500 \times (10.00 + 1.15) = \$5{,}575$$

Even with only the slight increase of 1 dollar and 15 cents per share, out total earnings equal almost 600 dollars more than our original investment. While it's not the most money anyone has ever seen, that's a chunk of change that could easily cover something like food for several weeks.

Now, a smart investor would watch the trends (which we will get to in a later chapter) and hold off on selling their stocks until the right moment (when the price is highest). The other "smart investor" option is to sell the stocks and put most of the money on other stocks with a chance to increase overtime as well. What you do with your earnings is ultimately up to you.

2. Hold on to Stocks and Let the Money Come to You.

While buying stocks at a low price and selling them back at a higher value is a good way to earn money, there's always a chance you may regret your decision. Your stock may not increase that much in value. Or worse, it may decrease after you buy it. You may sell it only to have it double in value the next day. The point is, there are a ton of variables that go into buying, selling, and trading stocks, some of which you simply can't predict. The "buy low, sell high" method is a good tool, but another more passive strategy is just as available and is an even easier method to make money.

That strategy is called "buy stocks and hold on to them." Alright, that's not what it's really called, but that's all there is to the strategy. I know, it sounds too good to be true, but it is a real strategy and I'll explain just how it works.

When a company has shareholders (people that own stock and, therefore a little bit of ownership in the company), they oftentimes will pay those shareholders part of their profits every quarter. That's right, companies will pay you just for owning at least one share. That's not too bad. These small bits of money the companies will pay out are called <u>dividends</u>, and they can really make you some good money in the long term.

Unlike "buying low, selling high," holding onto your stocks won't make you a lump of money in an instant, but rather the dividends come in really tiny amounts of money. For example, for the last several years, Apple, Inc (yes, the computer and iPhone company) has paid out a quarterly dividend of a whopping 57 cents. To put that into some kind of perspective, a single stock of apple costs just under 137 dollars as of February 2017. In comparison, 57 cents doesn't seem all that worth it.

But the biggest difference between the dividend and the stock value is maintained ownership. If you sell your Apple, Inc. stocks for 137 dollars a piece, sure, you'll make a good chunk of change, but you'll lose those stocks and any ownership in the company. Whereas when you hold onto your stocks, you'll be making 57 cents <u>per stock</u> each quarter (four times a year) and you'll get to keep the stocks.

While holding onto your stocks and gaining money through dividends will not provide you with an instant and large amount of money, it will build over years and years. Let's do a bit more math to really see the impact:

You own 500 shares of Apple, Inc. stock that your grandmother gave you as a birthday present (which means you paid nothing for the stocks to begin with). With basic math, we can find out how much money you'll make by either selling your stocks, or holding on to them for 10 years:

Number of Stocks x Current Value = Total money earned upon selling

Let's plug in our numbers:

500 x $137 (we're going to round up a bit) = $68,500

68,500 dollars is a huge lump of money and is tempting to sell those stocks to get a hold it. But, what happens if we don't sell the stocks and instead wait 10 years? Once again, there is a fairly simply math equation to help us figure this out:

Number of Stocks x ((Dividend amount x Quarters per year) x Years) = total amount made through dividends alone.

Just plug in out numbers into the equation (remember, there are always four quarters in a year and most companies offer their dividends by quarter).

500 x (($0.57 x 4) x 10) = $11,400

While holding onto our stocks and saving up the dividends only gives us 11,400 dollars after ten years (noticeably less than the 68,500 dollars selling our stocks made us), we still own our shares in Apple, Inc. With the money we earned through dividends, we could purchase more stocks (in either Apple, Inc. or other companies) to make even more money over time.

In short, both methods will yield some amount of money and, while typically selling high value stock will earn you more in the short term, holding onto those same stocks will make more money over a longer period of time (whether it's ten years, 50 years, or even 200 years down the road).

CHAPTER 2: PICKING THE RIGHT STOCK

As I mentioned before, there are tons and tons of different variables that determine if a stock will increase in value, decrease in value, or stay the same. Stocks can follow trends and show patterns as their values increase or decrease, or they may suddenly change with very little or no warning. So, with all of these different variables, how do you pick the stock that has the potential to make you money? There are a few different strategies that can help you decide on a stock:

Know the Basic Information Regarding the Company

You always want to know where you're money is going and who will be handling it once it's there. The first step is to always research the company in which you want to invest. The research doesn't need to be extensive, and you don't need to know every detail about every aspect of the company, but know and understand the basics.

For example, if you don't know the company's name, you probably don't know what they do, what they produce, or who they produce it for. Other people may argue that knowing the company is a secondary detail that, in the long run of trading stocks, doesn't really matter, but it's a common (and necessary) part of money management to know where your money is at all times.

For any and all companies from which you buy stocks, know what they do. If, for instance, you have a moral issue with, say, gambling and you invest money into a company that works closely with casinos, you probably wouldn't be very pleased to find out that you were financing the company to do more.

Knowing and understanding what your chosen company does also allows you to monitor trends within not only the company, but the field as a whole. Confused? Read the next section to fully grasp what I mean.

Look for Trends with the Stock

Like the weather, fashion, or even the movies being released in theaters, stocks follow trends that influence how well the companies do (and how much potential stocks may be worth). Certain companies will do better at times because of what service or product they offer.

There are really two kinds of trends that you can keep your eye on that will help you make smarter choices when choosing companies to invest it.

The first type of trend is simply the trend of the stock. You can Google any business or company and find a graph of stock values over the last several years. Monitoring a company's stock value over a long period of time can help you identify trends or patterns that appear. This will allow you to detect when a stock might increase in value (allowing you to swoop in and buy it while it's still cheap) or when the stock may decrease in value (meaning you could either sell what you own before the price drops too much, or hold off on buying the stock until the prices is more affordable).

Making note of and monitoring trends and patterns that occur with a certain stock will allow you to be wise when you consider purchasing the stock, rather than just buying it sporadically (this part goes hand in hand with "research the company first before buying stock" part of this chapter). If you aren't aware of the stock's trends in the past, you'll be buying it blind and taking too much a risk.

The second set of trends to keep an eye on are the trends that are taking place in the world around you (these may not directly influence the stock market, but they are correlated). Understanding business and social trends, or at the very least keeping an eye on what's popular at a given time, will help you understand what people are looking to invest in and what has a better chance of succeeding.

Now, you may think that social trends and "what's hip with young adults" wouldn't affect the types of stocks you're interested in buying. That is where you are so very wrong.

Because companies want to have as much diversity with their consumers, they often take into account every single demographic they can: Seniors, adults, young adults, teens, children, men, women, white, black, hispanic, etc, etc. The list can go one forever. Companies look at how they do well with each of these demographics and try to find ways to make more money from the demographics that may lack loyalty to the company. How do they do this? They research. They ask themselves "what are kids into these days?" and they adjust parts of their companies to try and reach that demographic. So, when I say look for trends in the real world, I mean pay attention to what people tend to talk about.

Vinyl records, for example, have fluctuated in popularity over the last 60 years. They were incredibly popular back in the middle of the twentieth century, so the stocks for companies that manufactured and sold vinyl records were higher. Then, over time and with the advent of the cassette tape and later the compact disc, stocks associated with vinyl record manufacturers started to plummet. Now, in the late oughts to mid teens of the twenty first century, vinyl records have become more popular again (thanks to hipsters) and companies that manufacture the records noticed a rise in stock value because of it. Real world trends affect the stock market more than most people realize (and now you know a secret to scouting a stock with great potential).

Diversify, Diversify, Diversify All of Your Investments!

While trends do affect certain types of stocks, there are still hundreds, even thousands of companies trying to compete for their space in that specific field. Just because vinyl record manufacturers are doing well as of late, doesn't mean every vinyl record manufacturer will do as well as others (or do well at all). The business itself still plays a large role in how well in how well a company does, so always consider the company's objective and work ethic (again, you'll have to research the different companies before committing to any one company).

Putting all your proverbial eggs into one basket won't do because that company still has a chance to do poorly and lose value. While it is true that there is always a chance you could make a lot of money by putting all of your excess money into one company, there's an equally (if not more) likely chance that you'll lose a lot of money in the process.

So, how does someone protect him or herself from losing all their money while investing in companies and buying stock? He diversifies where he invests his money.

Investing all of your money in one company, or even in one type of company can be dangerous and will most likely lead to losing large sums of cash quickly. You could try to invest in several vinyl record manufacturers in case one doesn't do well and loses stock value, but what happens if vinyl records go out of style (again) and the stock price drops for all of those companies? Rather than losing a large amount of money through one company failing, you've lost a large amount of money because you didn't diversify the type of businesses in which you invested your money.

Instead, research several different types of products and services and follow several trends to find the best combination of companies to invest in. Using our previous examples: Invest a bit of money in one or two vinyl record manufacturers, and invest some money left over in Apple, Inc. or another computer developer. That way, if one product begins to lose popularity and consumer demand (which is a large indicator of how well a stock's potential is), you'll have a second company selling a different product to make up for at least some of the loses you encounter.

Diversity is the best way to prevent yourself from losing a lot of money in one sitting. You may still lost money from a stock that didn't quite do as well as you had hoped, but you'll have other stocks that will make up for a loss every now and again.

Limit Your Options until You're Comfortable

Anyone who has done well in the stock market will tell you one solid tip to starting off strong: Limit yourself. Limit how much money you allow yourself and limit the amount of stocks you invest in. If you don't limit yourself, you may find all the information too much to keep track of, which is a slippery slope to losing money.

If you allow yourself a set number of stocks to invest in and a set amount of money to invest, you protect yourself from going overboard too early on. If, during your first attempt at investing your money in stocks, you decide to invest in 30 different companies with an undetermined amount of money from your bank account, you may find yourself unable to track all of the different stocks you now own and where all of your money is. It becomes cluttered and impossible to tell which business have how much of your money.

To start, set a limit that's easy to note and keep track of. Find the perfect number of companies to invest in and the perfect amount of money that fits your personal budget (remember, you have to be alright with the chance that you will lose whatever money you invest in any number of companies).

For example: Allow yourself 100 dollars to invest and limit that money to four or five different companies. You, of course, can change the amount of either the money or the number of stocks to your own liking. Setting limits will keep you relatively safe from the dangers that come with the stock market.

What's more important is to never, ever go past your limit. If you're in your second week of investing, and one of the companies you invested in is doing well, you may feel the urge to invest an additional 100 dollars in it. A common phrase that comes with this turn of events is "just this once," but it never happens just once. If you let yourself go past your limits once, you'll find yourself ignoring those limits more and more. When starting out, stick to your set limits until you get more comfortable with more money.

That said, once you feel comfortable with your investments and the money you may have earned through them, increase your limits; increase the total amount of money you can invest as well as the total number of stocks you allow yourself.

Be Passionate about the Company Succeeding

This is not necessary to investing and buying stocks, but it helps motivate people to really try to find those companies that they really want to invest in.

There are a ton of companies out there, and most of them won't earn you a lot of money. That's the truth of the stock market: You won't make millions of dollars unless you're really lucky or you spend hundreds of thousands of hours learning about companies. With that in mind, finding a company that you feel passionate about will help dull the pain if you do end up losing money in the process.

What do I mean by being "passionate" about a company? Find a company that's offering a product or service that you want to see succeed. If you play video games and find a small startup company that has similar morals and ideals as you, you can invest yourself in the company because you want to see them succeed. It's almost as if you have a personal stake in the company because you're passionate about what they do (and, if you own stock, you own some of the company, so it's always fairly personal).

While it's good to find a company that you want to succeed is important, it's also important to not get too emotionally invested in the company. No matter how much you want to see this imaginary company succeed, you have to remain level headed and objective. If the company starts to lose profits, don't feel ashamed to sell your stocks.

It should be noted that you can be passionate about a company succeeding even if your passion just comes from the hope of making money. Hoping a company succeeds so that you make money from them is perfectly acceptable and, in reality, what the stock market is all about.

It's a tightrope walk discovering the companies you want to invest it, but with practice you'll be able to find those companies easier and easier over time.

Find Companies that Offer a "Safer" Investment Opportunity

Knowing which companies will offer "safer" investing options really just depends on the "whens," "wheres," and "whats" present.

The "when" refers to the time of buying. Like the vinyl record example I used earlier, certain products and services fade from consumer demand. Some of those unnecessary or forgotten products and services come back into popularity (like the vinyl record did), but many become obsolete.

The "where" refer to the company's location in the world. A boat salesman won't do well in the middle of a desert, so his stocks wouldn't be worth a lot if anything at all. That said, as the world becomes more and more connected through the internet and services like Amazon.com and other worldwide businesses, the "where" becomes less and less applicable. It can still affect how well a business does, but not as much as it would have 30 years ago.

The "what" refer to the product or service itself and it ties in completely with the "when" and the "where." What does the company offer and is it demanded in the world today? Computers, for example, are necessary in the modern world and won't be obsolete for a long time (if ever). Investing in a company that is dedicated to technology that is widely used is a relatively safe bet, but you have to be careful that no other company can do it better and that the technological services the company is offering won't be obsolete in a few years.

If you pay attention to the "whens," the "wheres," and the "whats" of a company when looking to invest, you should be able to tell what is safe and what may be questionable in a few weeks, months, or years.

Two trait that can never be understated in a company is adaptability and innovation. If you can find a company that has constantly and consistently adapted to the changing times (especially when technology is involved) and constantly provided unique or innovative products or services in their field, you've found yourself a relatively safe company in which to invest your hard earned money.

Know How Many Stocks to Buy and From How Many Different Companies

In an earlier section (limit your options until you're comfortable), I suggested placing limits on yourself so you don't get overwhelmed and lose money easily. This is still true. Don't dive in too quickly (you have all the time in the world to learn). Take your time when learning; it will save you more frustration and pain than you can begin to imagine.

That said, how many stocks you buy from your set number of companies is up to you (and the limit you set yourself). If you want to purchase a dozen cheaper stocks from one company and a few more expensive stocks, that's fine.

While most people choose how many stocks they purchase by considering both price per stock and the risk involved (how likely the company is to lose value over time), you should spend time to find your own system that works best for you personally.

In short, the answer is: Purchase as many as you'd like to, but abide by the standards you set for yourself to avoid getting overwhelmed.

CHAPTER 3: HAZARDS OF THE STOCK MARKET

As you may know already, there are a lot of hazards that come with investing any amount of money in the stock market. Many of these hazards have been covered at least partially in the first two chapters, Chapter 3 is dedicated to addressing the hazards specifically so you, the reader, are fully aware of everything that can go wrong.

Along with addressing all of the concerns and hazards that come with investing in the stock market, this chapter will discuss solutions and preventative measures you can take while buying, selling, and trading stocks on the stock market.

There are a lot of Different Ways Investing Can Go Wrong

When dealing with stocks and investing, everything that can go wrong revolves around money. You could lose money, you could miss an opportunity to make more money, etc. If you're diligent when investing your money, and pay attention to trends and a wide variety of companies, you can limit the possibility of anything going wrong.

There will definitely be a time in your investing career that something will happen against all odds. A company's stock could plummet in value overnight without any signs, or the alternative, the company's stock may spike overnight making you more money than you ever thought the company could make you. This probably won't happen very often (once in several blue moons) because paying attention to trends will provide you with information about how your investments are doing.

Sometimes, however, losses will happen. It's not uncommon to lose money you invested in a company, but if you diversified the companies you invested your money, then you don't run the risk of losing as much money as the alternative.

Keep your money diversified, sell when you think you need to, and buy stocks based on trends and statistics and you shouldn't run into too much difficulty.

Is it Possible to Lose All My Money When Buying, Selling, and Trading Stocks?

It is and it isn't possible to lose all of your money in the stock market. I know, it's confusing, but hang with me for a second.

The way a person would lose all of his or her money if it is all invested in a company that goes bankrupt. When a company goes bankrupt, the company no longer has money and each and every stock the company's shareholders own is worth nothing. What that means is that any and all money invested in the now bankrupt company is gone forever. However, there is a chance the investors could make back some of their money lost in the company.

When a company goes bankrupt, it has to liquidate all of its remaining assets. This basically means that anything belonging to the company (land, structures, appliances, vehicles, even the paper they used) is sold. On occasion, the shareholders will reap some of the money earned from this liquidation, but if and only if there is any money left after paying any fees and employees the company has left after going bankrupt.

Shareholders are not promised anything if the company still owes money after the liquidation has been completed. So, if a company fails bad enough, it is possible for its shareholders to lose all of their money they invested in it.

Luckily, there are easy ways to prevent this from happening, though (all of which were covered in earlier sections). For started, diversify! Yes, I said it again. Diversify the companies in which you invest your money. Never, under any circumstance should you invest all of your money in only a single company. That is the biggest mistake any investor can make.

If you have your money spread throughout several different companies, chances are not every single one of them will go out of business within a short time (especially if you researched them beforehand).

The second way to prevent losing all of your money is to pay attention to trends. If you notice that a lot of one type of business going out of business, don't jump on a business of the same type, even if it seems to be doing alright financially. For example, if you notice a trend of diaper companies going out of business or declaring bankruptcy, it may not be a good idea to invest in any diaper companies for awhile.

Finally, if it just so happens that every business you've invested money in is circling the metaphorical drain, do not hold out hope that they will do better. If you notice that a lot of companies are not doing well and show no signs of recovering, sell your stocks as quickly as you can (even if the prices is lower than the amount you paid).

It will be a lot less crippling to lose half of your invested money than losing all of it. There will be times that you will have to take a loss. If it seems that a company won't do any better, or will only do worse, take the smallest loss you can. Sometimes it's all you can do.

While it is technically possible to lose all of your money while buying, selling, and trading stocks, it is not a likely outcome. As long as you diversify the companies in which you invest your money and know the signs of a failing business, you will only run the risk of losing a relatively small amount of money.

Always Know the Ways to Keep Your Money Safe

Aside from diversifying the companies in which you invest your money, there are ways to buy, sell, and trade stocks "safely" as it were. Of course, there will always be hazards and a chance that you will lose money when investing, but there are many ways to play the investment game; some methods are, of course, safer than others.

Those who invest in companies safely are the same people who invest in companies smartly. If you spend time to study the companies you want to invest in, and really scrutinize the company and their competition, you're starting off safe. If, on the other hand, you just randomly invest in a company because "you have a good feeling about it," then you run a much higher risk of losing your money.

In the case of investing, safe equals smart.

Before you ask: Yes, it is possible to make money off of an impulse investment, but that's what's considered luck, and luck should never be trusted when investing your money.

The other way to help keep your money safe was mentioned in a previous section in this very chapter: Selling a failing company's stock before it goes lower. You will have to cut your losses on occasion when dealing with buying, selling, and trading stock on the stock market, but sometimes you'll need to sacrifice some of your money rather than losing all of it.

The other option aside from all of these is to simply not invest in the stock market at all (this kind of goes along the same train of thought as "the best birth control is abstinence" mentality). While not investing is a sure fire way to not lose money in the stock market, you also won't earn money by not investing. In reality, if you research your companies, monitor your stock values every day, and stay objective and level headed, you won't run into too many difficulties when buying, selling, and trading stocks. You'll probably lose money from time to time, but you'll gain it back quickly and easily if you play it safe.

Know and Understand the Signs of a Bad or Unsafe Investment

Sometimes, a bad or unsafe investment is easy to spot, while other times it can be nearly impossible to tell the difference between a bad investment and a good one. Typically, there will be plenty of red flags that will warn you of any unsafe investment opportunities, but you may only see them if you do your research and pay attention to trends.

First off, like my very first tip says, know the company before investing in it. Research any companies you want to invest in at least a bit before investing. Even a quick Google search can save you from a lot of heartache.

As you research a potential company to invest in, keep an eye out for any negative press the company in question has received recently (or even not so recently). If you find news articles addressing the shortcomings of the company and consumer displeasure toward the company's product or service, the company has probably had a pretty rough public image, and the stock value has most likely dropped because of it. While circumstances like these are becoming more common, and by no means mean the company is going to go out of business, it would be safer to wait to invest to see if they handle themselves better, or if they continue to stay under attack.

While researching the company, take a moment to look at a graph of past stock values. Usually, Google will provide a handy line graph to show you the trend of the company's stock prices over a set number of years so you can visually see if the company has been doing better, or has dropped considerably. Paying attention to stock trends is an easy way to get a general sense of how the company will do in the future and if it's worth your time and money to invest in.

Speaking of trends (again), pay attention to those social trends still. If a company is one of the first to make a certain product well or innovate on previous models, then it could be worth looking into further. Using Apple, Inc. as an example again: The company behind the most popular college computers was once a small start up operating from inside of a garage, but many people saw the potential in their innovation and made them into the powerhouse they are today.

Paying attention to trends and innovations will help you better predict what might be popular in the future and have more consumer demand (which means more expensive stocks and more money for you).

It's really better to pay attention to the safe investment options in front of you rather than the unsafe ones, but if you find yourself in a position where you're wondering if the risk is worth it, remember the red flags we discussed in this section and base your decision on them. Sometimes, risks can pay off (but it's better to play it safe).

CHAPTER 4: TOP TEN TIPS FOR BEGINNERS AND PROS ALIKE

Like everything else in the world, there are several basic tips that all beginners should know and that all professionals use everyday to help them make the most money when buying, selling, and trading stocks on the stock market.

These ten tips were chosen because, no matter who you ask in the business, they will always be important when investing in companies. Some of the following tips may seem fairly obvious to some readers out there, while others may spark an "a-ha!" moment for others. Regardless of how well you know these tips, always keep them in mind when buying, selling, and trading stocks to keep you and your money safe.

Tip 1: Be Patient.

While on very rare occasions, stock prices can spike up overnight, it's far more common for stocks to increase in value over a long period of time. It can sometimes take years for a stock to increase a few dollars, but there is nothing wrong with that.

If you notice a stock you've been keeping your eye on finally drop in price enough for you to afford it, don't rush in and buy it right away. Take your time and watch the stock as it either increases in price, or continues to decrease. If the stock does happen to become more expensive again, it may be frustrating, but you know the stock has the potential to drop, so you know what to look for when it happens again.

Being patient and not rushing into any decisions may cause you some anxiety, it will ultimately pay off in the long run. Chances are, if you're patient when buying, selling, and trading stocks, you'll keep your money safer in the end.

Tip 2: Check your Stocks.

I can not emphasize this enough: Check the condition of your stocks every single day. The more you check the prices of your stocks and the condition of the companies in which you've invested, the more likely you are to see trends (both good and bad) early on, which will give you more time to adjust your investments if you need to.

Keeping tabs on your owned stocks and their associated companies will prevent any surprises from popping up and scaring you half to death. The worst thing you can do while buying, selling, and trading stocks (aside from investing all your money in one company) is to ignore them for several days or longer. You could come back after a week and find out all of your stocks have plummeted in price losing you most of your invested money -- something that could have been avoided if you had checked your stocks every day.

Finding time in the day to check your stocks doesn't have to be a chore. Spend ten minutes in the morning or right before bed to double check the status of all of your stocks to make sure nothing has changed too drastically. That's all you have to do. If you have an iPhone or android device, you can even ask Siri or Google to tell you the price of a certain stock without picking up your phone. It's that easy.

Personally, I prefer to be more involved. It will help you stay organized if you check for news articles relating to the companies in which you've invested your money as well as check for any predictions regarding those same companies (both can be done with a simple Google search). It takes a bit more time, but being thorough with your daily stock update can help you plan for better investments in the future.

Tip 3: Watch the News.

Watching the news goes hand in hand with checking your stocks everyday. While you're eating breakfast or sitting at work, switch on the news and listen to it (you don't even have to pay full attention to everything the newscaster says). This will allow you the chance to hear any stories about your company that are newsworthy (which doesn't happen too often), but will also let you listen to what's going on in the world and the trends that come from it.

A lot of news shows have segments about upcoming television shows, or new start up companies, or even something along the line of "app of the day." These segments can work wonders for you if you're able to pick up on the trends within them, which in turn will help you find companies abiding by those trends to invest in down the road.

Tip 4: Don't Listen to Friends and Family.

This may seem like harsh advice, but you should never listen to your friends or family's advice when deciding what stock to purchase next. Rather, don't *blindly* listen to your friends and family's advice. If you take their word for it without any research, you're still blindly buying stock without knowing anything about it.

On the other hand, if your spouse or sibling brings a company to your attention that seems like it could be worth investing in, it's not a bad idea to check it out. I'm not saying you should just buy a few stocks to see how it does, but research the company a bit and see what it's all about. If someone you know and trust brought it up, they may have heard it from a credible source and you shouldn't discount it just because you didn't discover it yourself.

Tip 5: Never Buy or Sell on Impulse.

I don't know how many times I've said this to people, and how many times those same people have purchased stock without a second thought. Always, always, always research a company before investing in it. Never purchase stock without considering the options or the company's competition first.

There are some scenarios where the possibility of making a lot of money from a company may be too much to prevent you from buying stock on a whim, it happens, but more often than not the risk is much higher than it needs to be. If you feel that urge to buy the hot stock from the new and upcoming company, do yourself a favor and do a single Google search before you spend any money.

Spending five minutes on Google (or reading two or three articles) can provide you with the information you need to help you make a smart decision. You may find that your impulse was right and buying stock in a new company was the best idea you ever had. If that is the case, congratulations! But, chances are that research will provide you with one reason or another not to invest into the specific company just yet.

Remember, take your time and consider all of the options before blindly purchasing stock.

Tip 6: Don't be Ashamed to Ask for Help.

Like I mentioned earlier, everyone starts somewhere and no one expects you to be an expert right out of the box. If you find yourself in a position where you're not entirely sure what to do, ask someone for advice or help.

Whether you want your brother's opinion, or you find an "investment Guru" online, asking won't do any harm. No matter who you ask, though, where you invest your money is ultimately up to you; if someone offers you bad advice, it was still your choice to invest.

Tip 7: Study.

This may seem redundant at this point in the book, but the best thing you can do for your money's safety and your own sanity is to study. Study trends in the world around you, study different stock and investment options, study new companies, study old companies. Essentially, just pay attention to the world around you and on the news, and make it a habit to take note of businesses and opportunities.

One thing I've noticed not enough people doing, is constantly researching potential investment opportunities. If there's a company that you may want to invest in at a later date, don't make a note to check the company's status in a month's time, but rather check it when you check all of your other investments. Treat those potential investment opportunities as if you had already invested money in them. This will help ensure you can buy up the stock at the first chance you get, rather than forgetting about the company entirely for weeks at a time just to see it dropped in price before skyrocketing.

Tip 8: Take Risks (But Only Sometimes).

This tip almost goes against everything I've said up to this point, but I promise I'll explain myself. Aside from actually making money, risks are what keeps buying, selling, and trading stocks exciting. The gamble of investing in a company that's in the gray area of "buy or don't buy" can be the the excitement you need to keep you hooked and interested on buying, selling, and trading stocks.

Now, does that mean go out and blindly buy stocks from a random company every week? Of course it doesn't! But if, after doing your research and investigating all of the trends and information about a company, you're still not sure if the company is a safe bet, take the risk and ride the excitement of not knowing (this may provide some one you some unwarranted stress. In this case, I suggest not investing in questionable companies). Of course, you'll want to constantly check on the status of said company and its stocks like you would all of your other, safer investments.

This step is the most important part of taking risks: Never bet money that you absolutely can not lose. Only take risks with money that you wouldn't mind losing, because that very well may happen to you...

Tip 9: Don't Rush into Investing.

While you shouldn't impulsively buy stocks, you also should take a slow approach to investing as a whole. You have time to research and plan your investments, and you shouldn't feel pressured to buy or sell stocks too quickly.

Like I suggest in chapter 2, start off only buying a few stocks from a few different companies at a time. Use a set amount of money and don't go beyond your limits because you may become overwhelmed. Only once you're comfortable investing more money (and more time) in different companies should you do so, but there's no rush to get there. If you own only 10 stocks for a year, there's no problem with that.

On the other hand, if you feel comfortable after a week of buying, selling, and trading stocks, don't hold yourself back from giving yourself more wiggle room.

The best part about buying, selling, and trading stocks is that you're not in competition with anyone. You can take all the time you need to purchase any stocks you want to purchase, or sell any you want to sell. Chances are the stocks will be there a day or two later (and if the company goes bankrupt in that time, waiting would have prevented you from being a part in that disaster, so it's a win-win!).

Tip 10: Practice Makes Perfect

Stock trading is just another skill than needs to be honed. Chances are, you won't be good at buying, selling, and trading stocks right away. You will probably downright stink, but that's okay! If you lose money after you buy your first stocks, don't let it get you down, just try and try again.

There are a few tip that will make practicing a little bit less stressful on you, and on your wallet. For started, don't use money you need. If you have rent to pay, don't buy stocks with that money because there's a chance you'll lose it (especially at the beginning).

When starting out, always use money you are willing to lose. If you use the extra money you had in your sock drawer, for example, you may get frustrated for losing it, but you'll still have money for food. Keep those priorities in check.

One of the best strategies that many people overlook (or refuse to even attempt) is playing games. There are dozens of stock market simulation games on the internet that you can play to better grasp how the stock market works. Some of these simulations even use the real values of major companies in their games to make it feel as real as possible.

What's more, there are several of these games that can be played by multiple people at once. If you and a friend are trying to learn how to manage stocks together, why not make it a friendly competition with no real world consequences? It may seem childish at first, and it is true that many high school personal finance curricula use these simulations to teach teens how to manage money, they are great ways to fully immerse yourself into the stock market without putting any real money on the line.

I strongly suggest www.howthestockmarketworks.com as a jumping off point. Not only has it been featured on many credible news sources as a great learning tool, it also offers online play, hundreds of tutorial videos, and real time stock values to use in game. Best of all, it's free to play!

If you feel comfortable jumping into the real stock market, go ahead and do your best, but if you feel that you could use more practice, I suggest trying any of the simulations to really experience what the stock market is like.

CHAPTER 5: MONEY MANAGEMENT AND THE STOCK MARKET

Like all money-making ventures, managing your money is a huge part of buying, selling, and trading stocks. Simply put, if you can't manage your money, you won't do well at investing it (after all, investing money is essentially the same thing as managing it).

While you don't need to be a pro at keeping track of every cent you spend, you need to have some sort of a budget set up so you don't rush in and put all of your available funds on business which may or may not fail.

Always have a set amount of money to invest. Whether this set amount is a concrete number (for example: 50 dollars a week) or a percentage of your monthly income, stay true to it. Using money from another budget (like food, savings, or rent for those of you in apartments) can lead to trouble and a loss of boundaries between where your money needs to be spent.

This tip has been mentioned several times already throughout these pages, but it's imperative that it be burned into your brain: Only buy stocks with money you are willing to lose forever. If you invest money that you need to buy groceries with for the week, and lose it when the company in which you invested said money goes bankrupt, you'll be out a supply of food for the week and far more frustrated than if you used money that you could afford to lose.

CONCLUSION

Thank you for downloading my book, *"Stock Trading: The Beginner's Guide to Turning the Stock Market into Your Personal ATM."* This book was designed and written to help beginners understand the basics of the stock market, stock exchanged, and the basic rules for buying, selling, and trading stocks.

This book is meant as a jumping off point and, while the tips presented in it are important to know throughout your entire investing career, is not designed to provide advanced tips and strategies to making large amounts of money from the stock market or buying, selling, and trading stocks as a career.

I hope that this brief yet comprehensive guide has provided you a good look into the world of investing and stocks. Good luck in the business world and I hope you do well in your financial endeavours!

INVESTING FOR BEGINNERS

Simple Investing Guide to Become an Intelligent Investor

By Sam Sutton
~~~

INTRODUCTION

Thank you for your purchase of *Investing for Beginners*.

The following chapters will discuss everything you need to know to become an expert in the world of investing. Investing your hard-earned money in the most prosperous places may seem daunting, but it doesn't have to be! With this simple and easy-to-learn guide, you can learn the ins and outs of investing in a variety of markets in no time!

With this book, you will be able to build a strong foundation that will lead you to feel confident in where and who you are investing all that green in! Don't just wing it, but genuinely learn it.

You will acquire all the knowledge you need to get yourself started in the realm of successful investing. Who knows, perhaps you are worth hundreds of thousands or more, and you just don't know it yet!

Thanks again for choosing *Investing for Beginners*. Every effort was made to ensure it is full of as much useful information as possible, please enjoy!

CHAPTER 1: WHY YOU SHOULD BE GROWING YOUR MONEY

You know what they say, "you have to have money to make money!" The same is totally true when it comes to investing. Endowing your hard-earned dollars gives you the power to put that money on a path to earning strong rates of return. If you don't invest, you are essentially missing out on awesome opportunities to increase your worth financially. While there is a chance to lose money when you invest, if you do so wisely, the potential gain is much more rewarding than the loss of never taking the action to invest.

These are the best reasons to invest your money starting now:

Cultivate Your Money

Obviously, the act of investing your money places it in a vehicle such as bonds, stocks, certificates of deposit, etc. These offer a return on the money you put aside to invest over a long period of time. These sorts of returns allow you to build your money, which helps it to grow to increase your financial wealth over time.

Build Your Retirement

When we are young and start working to make ends meet in the adult world, many of us do not even think about putting money aside for retirement. Many are unaware of their tolerance for risk, which inhibits people from considering putting money into investment avenues. The reality is, the greater the risk comes a better chance of earning a greater amount of wealth. The best places to invest your money when you are younger is in precious metals, businesses, real estate, mutual funds, bonds, and stocks.

Your mindset when it comes to investing should change over time, however. You need to become more conservative as you age, especially as you reach the age of retirement. You don't want to lose all that money you worked so hard to invest!

Acquire Higher Returns

If you desire to watch your money grow, you will need to invest it in places that have a high rate of return. You will earn more money the higher this return is. Many avenues of investment offer opportunities for you to earn high rates of returns. So, if you wish to earn a higher rate, you will need to do some exploring before investing your money.

Reach Your Financial Goals

Investing is a great method of reaching your large financial aspirations. When your money is earning a higher rate of interest, you are earning much more over time than you would by simply placing money in a savings account. The return on your investments can be used later in life to be put towards financial goals, such as buying a car, putting a down-payment on a home, starting a business, or getting your children through college.

Build on Pre-Tax Dollars

Some avenues of investing, such as employer-sponsored 401(k)s, let you invest your pre-taxed dollars. Having this option gives you the opportunity to save more money than just investing your post-taxed income.

Qualify for Employer-Matching Programs

There are a few employers out there that will offer their employees the chance to match the money you invest within your 401(k) up to a planned amount. The only way you can qualify for this opportunity is if you invest in your 401(k). This is the main reason many decide to invest in their company's 401(k) plans so they can gain the matching employer funds.

Begin and Build Businesses

Investing is a vital aspect of starting a business and expanding it. It also plays a role in helping other businesses expand. Many investors enjoy supporting entrepreneurs and devoting to the creation of new products and potential jobs. Investors truly love the part of their jobs where they can be part of the process in establishing contemporary businesses and assisting in building them to be successful that an, in turn, create a strong return on their investment.

Opportunity to Support Others

Investors sincerely like investing in other people, no matter if they are manufacturers, artists, business owners, etc. They feel good about helping other people achieve their goals.

Reduce Your Taxable Income

Being an investor allows you to reduce your overall taxable income by the act of investing pre-tax dollars into a retirement fund. When you generate from an investment loss, you can apply those losses against the gains you receive from other investments, which results in a decrease in the amount of taxable income.

Be a Part of a Brand-New Venture

New ventures are always in need of a backing of money. People starting new businesses look for investors to back them up. Investors like the thrill of being a part of creating something cutting-edge and being a part of something that introduces them to a whole new world.

CHAPTER 2: HOW COMPOUND INTEREST WORKS

By putting your money in a credit union or bank, you are paid a certain amount of interest for being patient and letting your money sit in their financial institution. You must change your mindset towards interest and view it as a great thing. When you take the action of putting money into an investment account, the interest made is working for *you*.

What is Compound Interest?

The act of compounding simply means that you are gaining interest on the interest that has already accumulated on an investment you made. It is the act of exponential increase of your investment. Compounding functions as a process of creating a return on an asset's reinvested earnings. It requires two vital pieces to work properly:

1. The reinvestment of earning

2. Time

View compound interest as a personal assistant that is able to help grow the investment you initially made. For those that are younger when they begin investing, compounding is by far the best tool, which is why it is highly recommended to start as early as you possibly can!

The Difference Between Compound Interest and Simple Interest

- **Simple interest** is received only from the earning of principal. For example, you have $1,000 that you were earning simple interest on at 2 percent each year, you would have made $20 a year on that

$1,000. Your interest for the first year would be $20, as would the second, third, fourth, and so on years. The amount you earned would not change. By the time 40 years rolls around, you will have made around $1,800.

- **Compound interest** enables one to gain more interest on the interest they are earning from an investment. For example, if you have $1,000 and earn 2 percent each year following the initial investment with compounding interest, the outcome is totally different than with simple interest. By the time you hit the end of your first year, you would have $1,020. By year two, you would end up with $20.40 instead of just $20. If you leave it alone for all 40 years, you will then have earned $2,200.00. That's more than $400 than utilizing the process of simple interest.

Creating Savings Over Time

As you can see, if you were to invest $1,000 in an account that only yielded 2 percent, your money would not grow at a very fast rate. The key to investing is constantly contributing money to that investment, which enables you with additional money that earns compound interest. The magical aspect of compound interest is that the more you contribute, the quicker you will see your money grow! Keep in mind that compound interest works better for you if you leave that money alone for a longer period of time. Again, a perfect reason to start early and build over time.

For example, let's say you are 25-years-old and you begin by investing $5,000 in a savings account. If you put $200 in each month during a span of 40 years, your money can grow as much as $158,900.00 by the time you reach the ripe old age of 65. If you contribute $500 each month for 40 years, you will have earned $380,700. But if you manage to start just five years later, you will only end up with $315,9oo+. See how starting early gives you the advantage of earning tens of thousands of more dollars?

Inflation

Another key aspect in the investment world is inflation, which has the potential to damage your potential for return. A good rule to follow when it comes to savings is to figure that inflation will be 3 to 4 percent each year. What this means for you is that you real returns will become eroded if your account fails to have a high yield. It is recommended to look for a savings product that offers higher yields in the first place, such as CDs, online savings account, etc.

Inflation may not be fighting against your yields at this very moment, but in the future, the rate of interest will likely rise. If you contribute more to your savings, you will find that your contributions will grow at a much quicker rate.

You Want to Earn Interest, Not Pay It

Compound interest is a pretty nifty tool, right? Beware, however, for it can function the opposite way as well.

Let's take a credit card company for example. A typical one charges around 20% in interest on unpaid balances each month. If you have an unpaid balance of $1,000, it will turn to $1,200 of debt by the time the year ends. You need to reverse the load of debt you have by applying the principles of compound interest. Transfer credit card debt to an interest plan with lower rates. Or, pick a loan with a yearly interest payment, instead of one with a monthly or quarterly required payment.

There are many investment vessels you can use to build up your compounding as well as maximize your efforts to build wealth:

High-Interest Savings Accounts

These accounts can be hard to come by, but by doing a bit of digging, you can find some awesome rates. If you are wanting to invest now, you should seek out banks that update their interest rates on a regular basis. Just a few percentage points can make a world of difference.

For instance, if you invest $5,000 in an account that grows 0.8 percent of compound interest within a period of 5 years, your return will be $5,200. But the same investment of $5,000 at a rate of 2 percent will yield you $5,500. For that extra $300, it is worth that extra time to locate a better interest rate to invest your money into. Bankaholic is a great start for consumers in the United States, and High-Interest Savings (https://www.highinterestsavings.ca/chart/) is a good choice for Canadian consumers.

Another good thing that brings you peace of mind is that the going rates on bank websites are often negotiable. Before you agree to a set rate, no matter if it is for a car payment, savings account, or load, ask the provider if they have any discretion. You might get an interesting look, but just for asking, the lender may just provide you the best rate available!

Certificate of Deposit (CDs)

CD's are very secure vehicles of investment, for they offer a fixed rate of interest till they hit a specific date of maturity. The advantage of CDs over high-interest savings accounts is that they guarantee that the interest rate will not change during the time you are investing. The catch is, your money is not liquid, which means you have to keep it locked away for a specific period of time. If you go to withdrawal it early than that date, you will have to pay a penalty. What you earn from the interest is also taxable.

There are various kinds of CDs and GICs (Guaranteed Investment Certificates). Each has their own set of terms, as well as pros and cons. As of now, CD and GIC rates of interest are about even with accounts that have high interest rates.

Stock Dividend Payments

Stocks that pay you dividends are a fantastic way to add additional income to your life. To grasp the absolute power of investing in these kinds of payments, read this example of the story of Grace Groner:

Grace was hired as a secretary after she graduated college in 1931. She worked for 40 years in this position. Grace did not earn an amazing salary as a secretary. She bought clothes from thrift stores and personal home sales and lived in a tiny apartment that was given to her after a friend died.

A few years later in 1935, Grace purchased a few shares of the company's stock that she worked for, at $60 per share. Her investment total was $200. Grace did not sell her share. Through the ways of share splits, dividends, and dividend reinvesting, when she passed away in 2010, her portion of the shares was worth over $7 million. By simply starting with $200, Grace was able to take full advantage of the power of compounding for roughly 75 years.

The Answer to Investing

By grasping how to maximize the usage of compounding interest, you too can harbor the power to create a substantial chunk of wealth over time. The vital key to keep in mind is that no matter how good or bad your finances are right now, you can change your financial future thanks to compounding.

CHAPTER 3:
THINGS TO KNOW BEFORE YOU INVEST

Many people never take the time to invest because they follow their belief of "my money is not safe within the markets." This is the conclusion many folks have, especially after the devastation the markets faced back in 2008. Stocks were sold, and many watched their 401k's become 201 and even 101k's. But now, those who had little faith in the markets before are started to get their feet wet in the world of investing once again. The stock market has since been doing spectacularly and proving all those skeptical journalists dead wrong.

Are you considering getting back into investing in the market? Well now might be the most perfect time to avoid the errors that many trap investors use to eat away at their gains. This chapter outlines how to invest your hard-earned money wisely with these valuable tips!

Know the Investing Costs

One of the biggest mistakes investors make is paying large amounts to invest their money. Stockbrokers, tax consultants, and financial advisors are not cheap and can easily eat away at any gains you receive within your investment portfolio.

The fees that Wall Street hides from investors is in the tiny print on your quarterly statements. And even if you were to take the time to read them, you would probably have a very hard time even understanding what they say. If you fail to learn what fees you are being charged with, you probably should avoid those services in the first place. Rule of thumb: if the fees are not completely clear and easy to understand, avoid them at all costs.

Here are the biggest sources of costs it takes to invest that you should keep in mind:

- **Inflation** is an ultimate killer of investment portfolios. If your gains of investment fail to keep ahead of inflation, you will lose money because the value of your money gets eroded away.

- When your investment advisor informs you how much you have made, they are more than likely talking about your gains before **taxes**. But the reality is, you never actually take home your pre-tax gains, just the after-tax ones. You must understand how the tax system will take care of your investments. You will also need to keep in mind what future development of the tax codes might be and how they will affect your investments as well.

- Mutual funds and brokers will charge you a fraction of the amount based on how big or small your portfolio is, which are known as **advisory fees.** Often times the number they charge is so small that you do not think much about it, but 2 percent can add up quicker than you think.

- Each time you sell or purchase a stock, a fee is charged by your brokerage, known as **brokerage commissions**. They are typically flat fees based upon either the amount of stock you buy or the trade. The lower, the better is the best way to go here.

Decrease Your Costs

Since you are now aware of the costs that can damage your overall portfolio, you are now in a place where you need to figure out methods of decreasing them. Here are the best things you can do to counteract those fees:

- **Invest in mutual and index funds that cost the lowest.** This obviously seems pretty straightforward, but many investors overlook this simplicity. There are very small fractions of a percent that can make a huge impact on your portfolio over many years.

- **Pay attention to cost changes.** Even though you invested in a low-cost fund, to begin with, does not mean that the costs will stay low. New competitors and products are introduced to the world all the time, which may play a role in increasing your fees.

- **Pay Capital Gains, not Income Taxes.** Active brokerage accounts or investment funds that generate many sales will also create high taxes on gains. You can reduce your tax costs by sticking funds that are passive and can make investments long-term. You will pay lower capital instead of those high-income taxes. Just be aware that some eliminated this benefit to investors.

- **Purchase Inflation Protected Treasuries.** To decrease becoming exposed to the inflation process, you can purchase gold, which has a tendency to go up in value when the value of money decreases. But this is not a practical method for the majority of investors. A simpler method is to put part of your overall portfolio in a TIPS, or a Treasury Inflation Protected Securities. While this will not shield you from collapses in the government, it can protect you from about everything else.

- **Invest in a Retirement Account.** If you are investing to mainly save up for retirement, ensure that you are utilizing an account that is also paired with tax advantages that let you avoid taxes not only now but in the future as well. This advantage can take you far, and the good news is that many big employers offer these accounts.

Gain Exposure to Upside Surprises

As an investor, you will get a first-hand look at how unpredictable the market is. This is a big problem for many investors because you are only allowed to invest for the gains you hope you will have in the future. As an investor, you are also a speculator for uncertainty in future events.

One way to handle all that uncertainty is to create a situation of upside exposure. What this means is that you should be willing to put money down on a number like you do when playing roulette. In other words, do not be stupid and make big bets randomly. Search and locate events that look highly unlikely, something that many others say is unlikely to occur. Make a small investment in that event, just remember that the odds are stacked against you.

For example, buying a $1 lottery ticket is not a good way to expose yourself to the upside of winning. This is because your investment of that dollar is too much for many jackpots in the first place. But if you purchase a lottery ticket with just a few coins of change, that would make more sense. The point here is, making riskier bets is perfectly fine as long as the cost to make them is low.

Diversify

Everyone has learned not to put all your "eggs in one basket." Diversifying your investments is vital. But many do not grasp how challenging it is to really diversify their money. Here are some pointers to get started:

- **Have more than one manager.** Many people think they are diversified because of the assortment of assets they had listed in their portfolios. The sad truth is many investors are exposed to a whole different type of risk, which is getting ripped off by their asset manager. Diversification should happen in every level.

- **Time preference.** Your investment portfolio should have assets in it that you expect to appreciate at different increments of time. This is a heavily overseen aspect of investing. Doing this helps you to avoid having those investments to be keyed in all at once, possibly during a time when the market could very well be crashing.

- **Mix assets.** You are not diversified if you own twenty or even one-hundred stocks and not anything else. You should strive to have a variety of classes when it comes to assets, such as treasuries, gold, bonds, stocks, etc. This makes you *truly* diversified.

Engage in Legal Insider Trading

If you hold a piece of valuable intel about an organization that you know others do not have access to, you should think about trading on that intel. There is nothing illegal about trading information that is secret that took you lots of hard work to come across. This is one of the best and only ways you can ever beat the market.

Here is the catch, however; do not do this if the intel that you withhold about an organization is one that you or a spouse works for. Do not act on this even if you hold an obligation to a third party. You can easily violate SEC rules when trading non-public information from a place of business you work for.

Don't Fall for "Hot Stocks"

Every single year some businesses run features in papers and magazines about hot stocks and sectors that are coming up. Honestly, you should never read these articles and avoid them as much as possible. The only thing these do is cause you distraction.

The same concept is true for investing in advice from people like Mr. Jim Cramer. When markets open the following morning, a stock that Cramer recommended is more than likely way to pricey. If you really want to place money in these hot stocks, wait a couple to a few months. If it goes down and you still think it is a good investment for your money, go for it. But the key here is to avoid that initial rush of wanting to trade by going for the bait of when it is first announced.

Ignore Most of Your Quarterly Statement (But Still Read it!)

Let's be honest, who really *likes* to read their statements in the first place? This is especially true when the market is not ideal. They will make you feel poor, ignorant, and can bring down your overall self-esteem when it comes to investing. But yes, you need to read *your statement*! You should not be reading them for your returns, but rather to keep track of those investing fees. Many brokerages and funds tap on extra fees in hopes that investors will not notice them.

Negotiation is Possible for Just About Anything

If you are signing on to investing in a sizeable fund, expect to pay the required fees. If you plan to create a brokerage account, however, you have a lot more room to negotiate what these fees are.

Financial advisors will say the fees are set at a certain rate and cannot be changed, but do not believe them. There is a plethora of fees offered by brokerages. The thing is, they are not obligated to find the best-priced ones for you. You need to negotiate with your broker to find the lowest fee they can. Once they give you a quote, simply tell them "these are not the fees I am looking for."

Invest in Passive Life Cycle Funds and Reinvest with Dividends

This tip can be a daunting one that takes some work, but welcome to the world of investing! The best thing you can do to set yourself up for success in the realm of investment is to invest your money in a lifecycle fund that is low in cost. These funds can change your allocation of assets as your age.

You should also take the step of reinvesting those dividends in your funds. Each year you should take the time to examine fees and every five years ask for assistance in analyzing your asset allocation. If you get divorced, buy a house, get married, have children, etc., you will want to re-examine these allocations.

You Will Never Be Able to Beat the Market

And you will not want to anyways! Here are crucial things you need to know when it comes to investing:

- Even if you were to learn how to beat the market, you could not beat it. If you try, you will more than likely end up farther behind than when you started.

- That being said, there really is no reason you should want to outsmart the market anyways. The great news here is that you do not have to fight against the market to receive gains from your investments. The real goal of investing is to save money for later in life and not let it lose value. Investing is not about getting rich quickly.

- Sometimes, returns will be a lot worse then you expect them to be. In the future, diversified investment strategies might not pay off as well. Changes in demographics, the spread of information, the age of the average investor, and declining markets have huge impacts. Never count on bonds and stocks to go up along a trend for forever.

CHAPTER 4: INVESTING IN STOCKS

Let me ask you this: Would you rather have $108,000 or $600,000? The answer for everyone is obviously the same! But how in the world can you as one person make $600,000?!

Well, start with investing $300, then add $300 monthly over the course of 30 years, and you will accumulate $108,000. But here is the difference when it comes to compounding at different interest rates:

- 2 percent = $147,600
- 5 percent = $245,600
- 10 percent = $620,700

The vital lesson to learn here is that saving is important, but what you earn on that saving is crucial to making more money with those investments. Sadly, in today's world, there is no method to earn anything close to that 10 percent when it comes to insured savings accounts. It is even challenging to earn 2 percent at times. The only method to get a higher rate of return is to take a risk and invest in stocks.

What Are Stocks?

Stocks are equity investments that serve as a part of ownership within a business. They entitle you to a part of that corporations earning and assets. Common stocks provide shareholders voting right, but no actual guarantee that they will receive dividend payments. The preferred stocks offer no right to vote but promise those dividend payments.

Shareholders receive a paper certificate of their stock, which is known as a security. This verifies the number of shares they own. But today, ownership is recorded electronically. This means that shares are held by your brokerage firm for safe keeping.

Stock investing can be awfully tricky. When it comes to successfully stock investing, you will need to get into a business mindset. Before you go out and purchase a stock, you should master all of the fundamental parts that make up investing. You will not become an investor overnight, but once you grasp the basics, you only then should be investing in stocks. This way, you have the confidence to make the right decisions.

Depending on how you measure stocks, they have averaged around 8 to 10 percent annually over the past century. Stocks always involve risk, which is why they pay much more than the average saving account. If you avoid risk, you create a whole new risk, which is not having enough money to adequately survive in your years of well-deserved retirement.

Stock knowledge is important! And contrary to popular belief, it is not rocket science.

The Rules of Investing in Stocks

Rule #1: Only Long-Term Money

Stocks would not even exist if they did not pay more than the alternatives that are less risky. The key phrase in this rule to remember is "over time." The longer your investment, the lower the risk when it comes to stocks.

Day trading is strongly risky because no one really knows what is going to occur each day. If you are not one to be extremely risky with their money, aim to invest in quality stocks because they show more value over time historically.

Rule #2: Moderation

Since the stock market is risky, it is vital to never put all your money in one place. If you are 25-years-old, for example, you should subtract your age from 100. This means that 75 percent should be put into stocks and the other 25 percent should be placed in savings.

Rule #3: Utilize Mutual Funds

Many people like purchasing individual stocks, but it is not necessary. You can function perfectly fine with a mutual fund as you lower your risk of reducing hassle at the same time.

Mutual funds are essentially a big pool of investments. It can be both a stock pool, which is a pool of stocks or a bond pool, a pool of bonds. Or, some mutual funds withhold both stocks and bonds, which is called a balanced fund.

Mutual funds allow you to spread the risk of investing in stocks by diversification among many stocks instead of just in a few. They also have people in them that do both the buying and selling and they keep track of the majority of that pesky paperwork for you.

Mutual funds fall into two categories:

- Index funds is similar to owning the entire stock market but is represented with an index. All the index fund managers have to do is buy the stocks, making it simple, and the fees minimal.

- Actively managed funds employ folks that claim they can outperform the indexes in index funds. They demand higher fees for their expertise.

Rule #4: Do Not Time the Market

You will quickly find yourself sitting on the sidelines if you try to time the market, especially when and if it takes off or crashes. There is a simple way to approach the stock market: with dollar cost averaging, which is also referred to as systematic investing. To do this, all you must do is invest in fixed amounts, such as $100 during regular intervals. This method works well because it automatically purchases more shares when they are cheaper, and fewer shares when they are more expensive.

Rule #5: There Are No Rules!

If you do not plan to take a bit of a risk, you will never reap the rewards. The trick to lessen the nightmares of investing is to be wise about it.

No rule states you must invest in stocks. If you dislike stocks, invest elsewhere, such as collectibles, peer-to-peer lending, side businesses, real estate, etc. There are many other avenues to beat the bank. While some involve more time and risk than others, their rewards can have the potential to change your life.

CHAPTER 5:
INVESTING IN REAL ESTATE

Purchasing real estate is a lot more than locating a new place to call a home of your own. Investing in real estate has been over time a progressive way to invest hard-earned cash and is a very prevalent investment vehicle.

The real estate market has tons of room to pocket huge gains by purchasing and owning. It is significantly more complicated than just placing investments into stocks and bonds.

Rental Properties

This is a venture that is as aged as the practice of owning land. People will purchase a property and lease it out to an inhabitant. The proprietor, known as the owner of the land, is then in charge of paying the loan, assessments, and expenses of keeping up with the property.

The proprietor charges lease to cover the greater part of the costs. A landowner may charge more since their goal to make a profit. However, the most widely used method is persistence, so they just charge enough lease to cover costs until the home loan has been paid in full, then the lease moves toward becoming a solid investment. The property may have appreciated in value through the time the loan was active, leaving the proprietor with a profitable resource.

There are, obviously, flaws in this seemingly "perfect venture." You can end up with a terrible occupant who destroys the property or you will end up having no inhabitant at all. This then leaves you with a negative income, leaving you to scramble to cover your home loan installments. This is why you should always opt for a territory where opening rates are low and pick a place that individuals will have to lease.

When you purchase a stock, it sits in your fund and over time, creates increments in value. When you invest in rental properties, many obligations come with being a proprietor. If the heater quits working, it's you who gets the telephone call. If you do not mind being a part-time and unpaid handyman, this may not bother you in the slightest. If you have the money and are willing to pay for these issues to be taken off your hands, it is a good investment to hire a property supervisor who would be more than happy to assist.

Real Estate Investment Groups

Real estate investment groups are similar to small shared assets for investment properties. If you wish to own a property to rent out, but do not wish to deal with all the hassles that being a landlord has to offer, a real estate investment group is more than likely a much better option.

An organization will buy or create a group of apartments or condos which then enable speculators to get them through the organization, they then allow them to join this group. A financial specialist can then claim one or various units of living space, but the people working the investment manage all of the units, which include dealing with upkeep, promoting empty units and meeting occupants. In return for this kind of management, the organization takes a percentage of the lease.

There are a few variants of investment groups, yet in a regular form, the rent is in the financial specialist's name and the units get together a bit of all the lease agreements to prepare for infrequent opening, implying that you will get enough to pay the home loan regardless of whether your unit is never actually leased out.

The nature of investment groups depends on the organization that is offering it. It is a protected method to get into real estate investment, yet many are still defenseless against expenses that frequent the mutual fund industry. Once again, performing adequate research is key to success.

Real Estate Trading

This is the intriguing and challenging side of real estate investing. Like investors who are miles away from a purchase, the land brokers are an altogether unique group. Land brokers buy properties with a goal to have them for a brief time, around three to four months. This is when they plan to offer their property purchase for an investment. This procedure is called flipping properties and is focused on purchasing properties that are either underestimated or are in an exceptionally hot market.

Unadulterated property flippers won't put any cash into a house for upgrades; the investment needs to have the incentive to turn a profit without adjustment or they will pass it by. If a property flipper gets captured in a circumstance where he or she can't empty a property, it can be damaging to the financial specialists as it would mean don't keep enough prepared money to pay the home loan on a property. This can prompt misfortunes for a land broker who can't offload the property in a terrible market.

An inferior of property flipper likewise exists. These financial specialists profit by purchasing sensibly evaluated properties and including an incentive by remodeling them. This can be a more drawn out term which relies on upgrades. The restricting part of this journey is that it takes time and just enables financial specialists to go up against one property at any given moment.

REITs

Real estate has been around since practically the dawn of time, where our ancestors who were cave dwellers began to chase out strangers from their space. It is no wonder that Wall Street has figured out how to turn real estate into a trade on an open market.

A real estate investment trust (REIT) is created when a trust, also known as an organization, utilizes a financial specialists' money to purchase and work salary properties. REITs are bought and sold on significant trades, much the same as some other stock. To keep up the status as a REIT, an organization must give out 90% of its benefits as profits. REITs are then abstained from paying corporate income tax, though a standard organization would be saddled by its benefits. After that need to choose if they wish to circulate its after-impose benefits as profits.

Much like standard profit paying stocks, REITs are a strong venture for securities exchange financial specialists that need customary wage. In contrast with the previously mentioned kinds of land speculation, REITs permit speculators into non-private ventures, for example, shopping centers or office structures and are exceedingly fluid. At the end of the day, you won't require a real estate broker to enable you to money out your venture.

Leverage

Except for REITs, putting resources into real estate provides a financial specialist a device that isn't accessible to securities speculators, which is the use of the REIT. If you are looking to buy a stock, you need to pay the entire estimation of the stock at the time your request. Regardless of whether you are purchasing on the boundary, the sum you receive is still substantially less than with real estate.

Many "traditional" home loans require a 25 percent down-payment that is contingent upon where you reside. There is a plethora of types of home loans that require just a tiny 5 percent. This shows that you can control the entirety of the property and its value by paying a small amount of the aggregate esteem. Obviously, the loan will, in the long-term, pay the estimation of the house at the time you purchased it, but you are still in control of the moment the papers are agreed on.

This is an aspect that encourages both the flippers of real estate properties and owners of real estate. They can make a temporary contract on their homes and put up front installments on more than one property. Regardless of whether they lease these out with the goal that inhabitants pay the loan or they sit tight for a chance to receive a greater investment, they are in full control, in spite of having paid for just a piece of the aggregate esteem.

The Bottom Line

We have taken a gander at a few kinds of real estate investing methods. Nonetheless, we have just touched the most superficial layer. Inside these cases, there are endless varieties of ways to invest in real estate. Likewise, with any venture, there are huge amounts of overall potential when it comes to real estate. This does not imply that it is a guaranteed gain. Make watchful decisions and weigh out all of the pros and cons of your activities before taking a dive into the real estate game.

CHAPTER 6: INVESTING IN BONDS

While the word "bonds" sounds awfully boring, it is far from it. They are a safe haven for retired and rich folks that do not wish to lose their money. Bonds play a role in your investment plan for other reasons as well. They help add diversity to your portfolio as they control risk. However, bonds can be a complicated subject to thoroughly grasp.

Bonds are completely different from sticks. Stocks that are well-selected tend to go up over a long period of time but can go down in the short run. Bonds also create a very nice steady stream of income that you can then reinvest or utilize for living expenses later on. Their price has the potential to fluctuate, but the overall bond remains the same. Plus, bonds like municipal ones can produce a tax-free income!

Getting Started with Bonds

It is crucial to understand the concepts of price, interest, maturity, and yield before jumping into making an investment in a bond. Small investors should really stick with high-quality bonds.

- Interest: The majority of bonds pay you interest semiannually.

- Maturity: When a bond reaches its maturity, they then have the power to pay the investor back at face value. Bonds that mature in two years or less are short-term ones, with 10 years being intermediate and 10+ years being long-term bonds. Most bonds are issues with 20 to 30 years maturity.

Types of Bonds

- **Zero-Coupon Bonds:** Many common bonds you receive interest payments every six months. But with zero-coupon ones, they credit you interest. However, it doesn't pay till it totally matures.

- **Uncle Sam's Bonds:** If you like peace of mind, these types of bonds are the essential way to go!

  - **Treasury bills** mature in a year or less with new ones being sold on a weekly basis. The minimum amount to purchase is $1,000. They are exempt from local and state taxes as well.

  - **Treasury bonds** take 10 or more years to mature. The minimum to purchase one of these bonds is $1,000.

- **U.S. Agency Securities:** Are similar to government bonds when it comes to safety, but be aware of the risks they hold as well.

- **Municipal Bonds:** These depend on which bracket you are when it comes to taxes. The higher the tax bracket, the more likely you will receive a better benefit than those that are issued by local and state agencies.

CHAPTER 7: INVESTING IN BUSINESS PARTNERSHIPS

Investing your hard-earned cash into a business is one of the best and most prevalent methods of investing in the journey of financial dependence for those small businesses. It is a great way to grow and create an asset that, when led under proper conditions, provides numerous amounts of cash those other investments cannot compete with. Small businesses grow through the means of representing the most crucial financial resource the family owns, other than their home.

Investments in business are built as either a limited partnership or a limited liability company. The limited liability is by far the most used, for it combines the best attributes of corporation and partnerships. When you are pondering over investing your money into a small business, there are two main types of positions you can choose to take:

Equity Investments

When you make an equity investment in any business, you are essentially purchasing part of the overall ownership, or in other words, taking a piece of the pie. Equity investors give capital with cash in exchange for the percentage of both profits and losses.

The business then can utilize this allotment of money for a variety of things that are business related, from funding expenditures, the running of daily operations, decreasing debts, purchasing other owners, creating liquidity, or hiring new employees. This type of investment when it comes to small businesses results in bigger gains but comes with a bit more risk. If expenses become higher than the amount of sales, the losses get handed over to the investor. If things go well, the return can be exponential.

Debt Investments

When you make a debt investment in a business, you are loaning money in exchange for repayment of your loan down the road, along with income made from interest. Debt capital is given in the form of loads with amortization or the purchasing of bonds that are issued by the business itself.

The biggest advantage to debt investments is that you get a nice cozy spot in the structure of capitalization. This means that if the company fails, the debt takes priority over stockholders, also known as equity investors. The highest level of debt incurred is a first mortgage secured loan that has a lien on a piece of property or an asset that is very valuable, typically the brand name.

Which Type of Partnership Investment is Better?

When it comes to life in general, especially when it comes to the subject of businesses, there is no simple or clean-cut answer. For example, if you were an early investor of McDonald's and purchased equity, you would be very well off. If you had purchased bonds with the debt investment method, you would have earned a decent amount in return, but by no means as spectacular as the other.

Things to Know Before Investing in Partnerships

- **Beware of the opportunity** by asking why the opportunity is available for investing in the first place. Usually, businesses are trying to raise money, which usually means they failed to get a loan from a bank. You need to find out the story behind their reasonings.

- **Understanding the structure** can help you to determine how the legal systems and the IRS view the profits and liabilities of the business you are considering investing in. There are major chances that the business could fall out. You can be responsible for bills that are unpaid or other liabilities depending on the structure of the business.

- **Keep in mind that you may not see returns for years,** so do not assume that investing in a business will equal automatic profit. Startups especially need all the money they can get, with earnings usually being added back into the business. Returns for investors may not be present for 3 to 5 years or more.

- **Have an exit strategy planned** just in case it takes too long for you to see solid revenue from your investment. You do not want to burn through all your investment before a business opens its doors.

- **Do your homework** before investing your money into a startup business. You want to know the background of the business and have a good understanding of it and its competition. You should also request a business plan that includes a description, financial plan, market analysis, etc.

CHAPTER 8: INVESTING IN PRECIOUS METALS

Investing in gold and silver is quite simple, as well as fun and highly profitable. Almost anyone can learn how to begin purchasing gold and silver as a physical way to wealth. Gold and silver, along with other precious metals, have the strength to hold their value, which can mean not only a beautiful but a long-term investment as well.

The process of purchasing, selling, and holding precious metals involves some annoyance that you need to understand to be successful and gain awesome returns.

What Are Precious Metals

Precious metals are naturally occurring, rare, and challenging to find than other metal types. The rarity of these metals gives them high economic value. They are still valued for their use in commodities, jewelry, art, and investments.

- Gold
- Silver
- Palladium
- Platinum

Precious Metal Investing

Precious metals are highly valued in many industries, so they are traded on a regular basis in world commodity markets. People in all countries have some sort of need for precious metals, which means they are constantly changing due to the supply and demand for them.

These metals can be bought by people as investment vehicles. This is done through a mint or a broker, in which it can be purchased in a few formats, such as in its physical form, stocks, mutual funds, ETF funds, etc. Those that choose to buy precious metals in their physical form usually purchase bars, bullion, or coins in various shapes and sizes, depending on the amount they purchased.

Inflation is a common risk when it comes to investing in metals. Buying them at the present time at the current price protects their value against future metal inflation, which is why they make for ideal investment vessels. This is certainly true with gold, the most popular investment metal due to its high value and availability.

Buying Precious Metals

Investing in precious metals is a great method if you are looking to make quick profits and increase your savings for future living. You can purchase or sell small to large amounts of metals on a regular basis to make money daily. You can also buy small to medium allotments to hold as a part of a retirement account.

The best metals to buy are silver and gold because they are the ones most often used as currency. You will need to talk to a stockbroker or a dealer of precious metals to buy them. You also will need to do adequate research on the various methods of precious metal investing to discover all the methods in which you can gain a profit from each precious metal individually and together.

CHAPTER 9: INVESTING STRATEGIES

When it comes to investing, any amount of knowledge adds significant value to you as a growing investor in the market. This chapter is loaded with strategies to help you invest the best you can as a beginner in the world of investing.

Don't Wait, Start Now

There will never be a better time to begin the investing process. Don't wait till you get a higher paying job or save enough money. If you are a procrastinator, this will never come for you. Start now, with a little from each paycheck you receive. The quicker you start, the better you will be and the bigger of an investment you will incur over time as it matures.

Expert Advice

Experts in the investing world can help you to understand all of the investment options that are open to you. You will be able to determine which avenues of investing are right for your lifestyle with the help of an investment planner. Many are free! Open an account and link your accounts.

Start Out Simple

After you are knowledgeable about the options you have, it is recommended to start with the simplest and learn the rest as you gain experience. You can make mistakes and not feel bad about it when you are just starting out, with small investments like $100.

Know Your Goals

Before you make the step to invest, know what your goals are for venturing into investing in the first place. Do you want to start saving for retirement? Do you want to grow a fund for your kid(s) to go to college? Investing is much different from just saving money, it is a long-term process.

Know Your Options for Investment Vehicles

Make sure you plan out what you wish to invest in as well when deciding your goals. You can invest in brokerage accounts, college funds, 401k's, etc. Some of these have big tax breaks that will make them a clear advantage.

Open an Investment Account

Once you have made a clear decision about what vehicle you wish to use and what your goals are, it will be much easier to sign a form and get funds rolling into an account. Make sure you have a reliable platform to buy and sell your investments.

Start in Auto Investing

You should start this as soon as possible with regular contributions. Many brokerage accounts totally support monthly investment options.

Learn a Hands-On Approach

Many people think that once they make an investment, they just let it sit there and it will do the hard work for them. It is vital to track your investments to check to see if they are growing. Make it a priority to check into them every six months to a year.

Picking an Amount to Start Investing

This will be a major decision when it comes to handling your budgets and the increments you will make to your investment over time for it to grow substantially.

Make Investing a Habit

To increase your investment earnings over time, you have to stick to it and contribute regularly. It's kind of like a plant; if you don't water it and provide it with a light source, it will eventually die and not create any produce for you to pick.

Make Baby Steps

Don't expect investments you make to make anything extraordinary any time in the near future. You must learn to be patient and look into other investment options to invest money in as you wait for your others to grow over time.

Be Knowledgeable of Packaged Mutual Funds

This is a great option that many beginners in investing overlook. They are less risky and are quite volatile. The costs for transactions are also low, and every fund is easily managed by portfolio managers who are in charge of rebalancing your portfolio to ensure that proportions are consistent with your investment.

Be Wise When Choosing Stocks

You will never be able to accurately time a stock market, but they are a good option and don't require you to have a lot of capital upfront. If you pick wisely, you will have a peace of mind knowing you will have a stable income.

Take the Time to Learn

It is no secret that there is a lot of information regarding investing. If you are serious about becoming a seasoned investor, go out of your way to purchase investment books, strategize with the investment knowledge you gain. Look online and perform research, checking out companies that peak your interest. Ensure that you are fully aware of what those companies are earning, who their customers are, and more.

Play Safe

Investing is not the time of place to be wild with your money. Make a margin of safety for yourself, but be sure not to be too over-dramatic with your boundaries, as it could keep you from exploring other vehicles of investing or keeping you from taking the risks that are required in investing to reach success.

Don't Impulse Invest

Make sure to always take your time and speak with experts before going out and purchasing stocks, bonds, funds, or another other investment vehicle.

Beat Inflation

No matter what you choose to invest in, try your best to beat the rate of inflation, or you might find that you are losing money rather than gaining it. Simply placing your hard-earned money in a savings account is not a method of investment, but an easy-way-out of doing the hard work to reach your financial goals.

Create an Emergency Fund

Before you go out and start the process of building up your investment empire, make sure to create an emergency fund first. Also, it is a good idea to create an insurance cushion that will protect your money. You never know where the road to investment will lead you.

CONCLUSION

I want to congratulate you for making it to the end of *Investing for Beginners!*

I give you a big pat on the back for reading the entirety of this book, for you are one giant step closer to becoming your very own investor! While money can't buy happiness, it can sure help to build a cushion that brings you peace of mind when life gets a bit rocky. Wouldn't you rather be prepared than sorry?

As you have learned, everyone should learn the basics of investing. Now that you have soaked up all this valuable information, you should feel all that confidence bursting at the seams inside of you. Yes, you can even learn how to invest like the big guys on Wall Street with a bit of basic knowledge, common sense, and a bit of faith in the market.

I hope that everything in this book has given you the information you need to take the next step in investing some of that hard-earned money of yours. All the tools you need to achieve your investment goals can be found in this book as a reference if you get a bit lost.

Good luck my investing friends! Make that money grow!

If you found this book useful in any way, please take a moment from your investing ventures to leave a review on Amazon. It is always appreciated!

TRADING FOREX

The Basics You Need to Immediately Make Money from the Forex Market

By Sam Sutton
~~~

INTRODUCTION

I want to thank you and congratulate you for downloading *Forex: The Basics You Need to Immediately Make Money from the Forex Market*.

    I've always had a passing interest in economics. From keeping up with the latest blogs to listening to my favorite economics podcasts, economics has been intriguing to me for years. For years I also heard about the various markets of exchange where traders could make money. Bonds, stocks, options and Forex were a staple of the programs that I listened to and the blogs that I read. After hearing so much about the Forex market, I had a sudden thought that brought me to start investing, who exactly invests in the Forex market? It was in discovering the answer to this question that I realized you don't need to be a trained or seasoned investor to get started in Forex; you just need to have the will to learn and the discipline to execute trades with patience.

Over the last two years I have gone from having a causal interest in Forex markets to gaining over half of my income this year through Forex trading. My foray into Forex was not without its challenges, but with the knowledge that I have gained, I want to make investing and profiting in Forex as simple a transition as possible for you. I will teach you the key pieces of information that you need to know so that you can start trading right away. Whether you want to take an analytical approach or a news and policy approach to trading, I will teach you everything you need to know so you can get started right away.

If you decide to approach Forex but miss the essential lessons I offer then you will be starting in Forex at a huge disadvantage. Forex trading is more than just making a few good calls – it's about understanding the mechanics of trading and knowing when to pull back trades or when to increase your total investment. Trading is a marathon, not a race; I want you to be successful in Forex trading not just in the immediate, but also for long into the future. Without the knowledge that leads to consistency in profits, Forex is little more than an attempt at legalized gambling. You can take the gambling approach, but I know that with just a few lessons you will be in a place where you can find success in the long run.

It's time to make a change in your life; it's time to get invested in Forex. There are opportunities to make money at any time of day from your home, but these opportunities are hidden behind knowledge of skills and an understanding of the markets. This is what I offer, the skills to make intelligent trades that will allow for long term success in Forex trading. Continue reading and soon you will know all of the necessary information to grant financial freedom for yourself and your family.

Sam Sutton

CHAPTER 1: THE BASICS OF THE FOREX MARKET

Faith, Currency and Gold

If anyone discovers that I have a love for economics, I usually get a cold or confused response. The reaction all comes form the sentiment that economics could not possibly be interesting, but I believe this is merely because economics is often framed incorrectly. So much of modern economics is thought to be extremely mathematical, and while this is certainly true, economics wasn't always this way. At one point it was more about the study of how humans that don't know each other interact. It is the study of relationships that form around a center of money. I start with this concept because as you begin to trade in Forex, it's important to understand both how the Forex market works and how we came to rely on this system. Understanding these fundamentals have helped me grasp the interplay between countries and has improved my trading overall.

The global Forex markets as we know them today are very different from how currency prices were determined just fifty years ago. You know that Forex markets control the pricing of different currency, but before the currency system countries relied on a gold backed system. There are some that would claim a gold backed system is better than what our economy currently uses, and while there are some merits to this system, our current global economy is far better at handling financial crisis due to a key change in the monetary system of most large economies. The gold system was merely adopted first because of the rarity of gold, and because it is inherently an easy system to understand.

For a moment, consider a piece of currency that you have on you. Whether that note is a twenty dollar bill, or merely a quarter in your pocket, ask yourself; what gives this coin or bill value? It's a simple question but one that is actually quite complicated in the abstract.

Before the current financial system the value of your dollar was merely a placeholder for gold that the United States held. The gold of the United States was essentially disturbed around the country through the form of their minted currency. The economy of a country was therefore highly dependent on that nation's supply of gold. If you think back to your history classes in high school and middle school, you may realize that much conflict over the last millennia had roots in obtaining more gold from foreign powers or new land that had not been claimed. This system is simplistic in how it works – it's fairly simple to realize that the currency in hand supplements gold, but it also makes for a lot of difficulty in terms of currency conversion.

For centuries the best way to convert currency was not to go through a government institution, but rather to go through large banks that issued their *own* currency. This currency was a note that allowed traders to use their hard earned money across multiple nations. The banks that ran this system profited immensely, as they were providing a much necessary service that government institutions were simply not handling as well.

The question about what gives your money value is simple in terms of the gold standard, but we can see problems in terms of generating real wealth on a level of nations, and also that exchanging currency was highly problematic, often requiring third parties to handle currency exchange through their own intermediary currency. Today's system is far better, but the answer to the question of valuing currency has changed greatly. In simplest terms, the currency that you have on your persons is valuable simply because you think it is valuable. There is no gold backing your dollar bill; it cannot be exchange in value of any precious metal (dollars used to be exchangeable for gold). The value of the dollar is a collective agreement across the world economy that the dollar is worth something. Understanding this premise that currencies today are largely based on a faith based system, you can start to see how modern currency exchange works.

There's a reason I asked about the value of the US dollar specifically; it is the currency that all other world currencies are traded in. Meaning that if you want to buy Euros or Chinese Yuan, you will be making a transfer in US dollars. From this initial transfer, we have the Forex markets starting to take shape. As currency is traded back and forth, the respective volume and demand of currency is what shapes their value, along with the interaction of various national banks and institutions that can change the money supply. For example, the US dollar's value is based on three inputs: one, that the dollar inherently has value as a tradable item and is recognized across the world. Two, the dollar's value is based on its trading volume and how in demand it is relative to other world currencies. Three, the Federal Reserve has the authority to print money, and this will reduce the value of individual dollars through inflation. Through these three inputs, partially based on faith, the rules of supply and demand and the whim of a government body, we have our modern Forex system.

For your part, you will be making money off of the fluctuations in currency. We'll be getting into the specifics of how currencies are traded, but to give you a simple idea of how you will make money, let's work with a simple example. Suppose that you were to go on a trip to Europe – anywhere in the Euro-zone that accepts the Euro. Before your trip to Europe, you decide to exchange some spending money so that you go shopping and go out to eat. This transaction is an example of a currency pair, in this case the USD/EUR currency pair. If you decide to exchange 500 dollars to Euros, you would currently get 463.59 Euros. The rate of transfer here was 0.93, meaning that for every 1 USD you were provided 0.93 Euros. On the way back to the United States, you realize that you made all of your purchases through your bank card, and that the total amount of 463.59 Euros are still in your possession. You decide to exchange this money back for US currency on your way back to the United States. The transfer of 0.93 has changed, and is now 0.91, meaning for every US dollar you receive 0.91 Euros in return. In this case, the USD has decreased in value relative to the strength of the Euro. When you make your exchange back you are left with 509.44 USD. That's right; in this trip you managed to make ten dollars simply through the fluctuation in the currency rate.

This simple demonstration shows a lot of the specific ways in which foreign exchange currency works. You always purchase currency as a pair, so you are trading on the strength of one foreign currency versus another. Currency pairs are standardized, as is this one: USD/EUR. As the ratio increases, the value of the USD goes up and the Euro goes down. As the ratio decreases, the Euro gains in strength and the USD depreciates. This small-scale example is exactly how Forex works – you make a bet on a currency, hold that currency for some period of time as the price exchange changes, and then sell that currency when you are able to make profit. There are many ways of determining the ideal currency pairs to buy into, but regardless of the strategy, the method to profit is always the same.

The Value of Forex Traders

Forex message boards are a great place to reach out to other traders and learn information about the markets. It can be difficult to find the most useful information on these boards, and some questions certainly come up more often than others. One of the most common topics on these message boards pertains to the value that traders grant to Forex. When you think about what the role of a Forex trader is, it is hard to come away with the idea that they are anything other than speculators. This term, 'speculators' has a negative connotation to it, and I wanted to clarify a bit where the value in the economy comes from with Forex trading.

I gave a simple example of how you can make a profit through Forex with the exchange of dollars for Euros and then back again. The change in the conversation rate was precipitated by the supply and demand of each currency on the Forex market; meaning traders were responsible for the ten dollars of profit in this currency exchange. Why they happened to increase the value of the Euro versus the dollar is where the traders' real value comes in; they are setting the exchange rate for more than your trip, they are also determining the price of imports and exports in a country. In this example, it became cheaper for Europe to purchase items from the United States, specifically because their currency now grants them more USD per a single Euro. This change in their purchasing power allows for more output from the United States because their products are more competitive on a global scale. All of this is due to the work of currency speculators working in their own interests. By trying to determine the value of a currency in the future, all Forex traders work together to set the market rate for currency exchange, and in turn facilitate global trade by setting fair prices for exchange.

If the value that you offer by trading on Forex is still not clear, I want to leave you with one last thought, the power of markets. Imagine if it was the single responsibility of someone to determine the world's currency prices. This would be an immensely difficult job, as it would be up to a single person to determine values based on so many inputs that his or her job would be nearly impossible. When dealing with so much information that could influence the price of a currency, you need thousand of people working in coordination and sifting through all of the different factors that could determine currency prices. The point is that the work of the collective that individually is working in their own self interests, provides a better value for currency prices than any government body or single entity working to regulate the market. The value of the individual trader is that they are added to this collective of information that is determining the value of the currencies across the market.

CHAPTER 2: REQUIREMENTS TO START TRADING

Broker

You will need a broker to get started with currency trading. There are two schools of thought to how you should select a broker. You can either go with whomever has the lowest rates and a wide consortium of currency pairs to trade, or you can pay a little more to have access to research specific tools offered by particular brokerage houses. It is my strong suggestion for beginners that you merely go with the cheapest brokerage house. Even small firms will trade at least forty or fifty currency pairs, with the larger markets trading around ninety. This is not a function of the cost of the broker, but rather selecting one based on size and influence. Paying for advanced brokerage tools is the main driver in higher fees, but these tools will not be of us to the inexperienced trader. Also, it is dependent on a particular style of trading that you may not gravitate towards. Go with the cheapest broker, learn how to use their specific tools for analyzing currency pairs, and then move to a more expensive broker in a couple of years once you fully understand how analyzation tools should be used. This is a mistake that I've seen a lot of traders make, where they will use expensive tools but will not quite understand all of the measurements. In depth analytical approaches take years to master, and a long time to simply learn how to understand the resulting data. Early on, you will be using easier analytical strategies that won't require such computation.

In order of brokers that I would recommend, please refer to the following list. None of these brokers offer extensive research tools, but they have a wide variety of currency pairs and their rates are extremely moderate. Also, as you are starting out I understand that you might not have the largest investment pool, as such there are some brokers that have heavy minimums while others will have no minimums at all – this by itself might be the determining factor in choosing your broker.

Oanda	(No Minimum)
Ameritrade	($2000 account minimum)
FOREX.com	($250 account Minimum, only 50 currency pairs)
FXCM	($50 account Minimum, only 39 currency pairs)
ATC Brokers	($5000 account Minimum, only 35 Currency pairs)

Capital Requirements

Making money through Forex markets is not a race; it is a marathon. To ensure that you have the right amount of capital and that each trade you make is not eating too far into your investment fund, we have one simple rule: the 10% rule. This rule will allow you to trade long into the future, by ensuring that no single investment is too large to maintain. As you are starting out, I suggest that you do not use any leverage, meaning that you do not buy any currency on credit. In addition, you should start trading with $1000, with a $3000 account really necessary to make any significant amount of money through trades. Remember that brokers' commissions will eat into your profits, so you will want to make trades between $50 and $100, at a minimum. Nothing is more disappointing than making a great trade but not making that much profit because your investment pool was not large enough.

If your investment fund is not on par with the sizes I described, then you will start to run into the temptation of spending more than 10% on a single trade. With the ten percent rule, you are encouraged to at most spend $100 on a $1000 account. If you are starting off with $250, even a $50 trade is more than twice what you should be comfortable with. The plan is that you are successful with about 70% of your trades. If you accept that 30% of all trades will either net you zero profit or possibly lead to some losses, then this ten percent rule starts to become really important. As you start to set up your investment fund, make sure that you can take on this risk and that you are prepared to only spend ten percent of your fund on any single transaction.

Understanding Your Investment Fund

There is a mistake that I see a lot of traders make – they do not create a salary for themselves based on their profits from Forex trading. This is a rather basic idea about savings, but your venture into Forex markets is similar to an independent job. Working alone, you are going to have to manage your investment fund as if you were the boss of your own company. It is important therefore that you separate your investment fund from all of your other finances. Your investment fund should be considered for one thing, Forex trading and nothing else. You cannot draw from this fund to pay rent, buy food or even consider it your retirement account. It must be fully separate from all other savings accounts, including emergency accounts and college funds.

The second aspect of your investment fund is that you should always be working to increase the size of this fund, not because you want to use that money immediately, but so that you can increase the maximum size of your trades. As your investment fund increases, so does the maximum that you can trade according to the ten percent rule. Your goal then for making true profit and holding onto that profit should come from a salary that you pay yourself based on your investment fund. Over the last two years I have seen my investment fund grow much larger, and in that time I have paid myself roughly 20% of the total growth of the fund. 80% of the profit that I make from trading goes right back into the investment fund, allowing for continual growth in my profits. I believe that you must think about your investment fund this way, and that you must separate it from your paid out profits and any other funds that your household may have.

Understanding the Time Commitment

Depending on the strategy that you use to approach Forex markets, Forex may take up a few hours of your week, or it could take a few dozen hours. The two basic strategies rely on either a value trader or a day trader mindset. The main difference between these two is the time commitment to trading. A day trader needs block hours to commit to trading, so think about trading for six to eight hours in a single session. A value trader makes a trade and holds onto it for several days, weeks or months, meaning that they just have to do the initial research up front, and then can monitor their investments every week. As you start trading, you are likely to do a mix of both. Unlike day trading in other markets, Forex offers the unique ability to be traded at any time of day. There will always be currency markets that are open to trades, regardless of where on the planet you call home. You may need to trade late at night to get those block hours for trading, but this is one of the fastest ways to profitability.

Within two or three months, you will have a sense of the type of trading that leads to the most profit, and then you will have a much better sense of the average weekly time commitment. In short, plan for around ten to twenty hours a week to start, and as time goes on and you find the strategy that works best, expect this number to either go up or down. I know many traders that now work on Forex full time, so if your profits come in at a nice rate, this may also be an option for you, allowing for enough time in the week to focus on day trading or research for value trades.

CHAPTER 3: THE MECHANICS OF TRADING

Knowledgebase

Like any industry, there are industry specific terms to Forex that are essential to start trading. These are just terms that the industry uses for common measurements and to facilitate faster trading. Make sure that you know what each of the following terms are and where they fit into the larger picture of trading on Forex – this is the essential knowledgebase you will need to start trading.

Pips

A Pip, or pips is how traders refer to movement in Forex holdings. One pip is a movement in the ten thousandth decimal place, or .0001. If the currency pair USD/EUR moves from 0.93 to 0.9350, it is said to have moved fifty pips. A pip is not a complicated concept, but rather is emblematic of how currency pairs shift in price. They move in very small increments and this is the most significant decimal place that is worth noting. Currencies fluctuate at smaller rates than a pip, and at times several thousand greater than a pip, but the pip is the most basic measurement that we have when it comes to an individual currency pair.

When looking at currency pairs, you will see changes measured in pips. In addition to just a handy metric, you can also use this to demine your profitability minus broker fees. For example say the USD/EUR is trading at 1.1, and then has an increase of 27 pips, or changes to 1.1027. In this case the US Dollar increased in value. If you wanted to determine your total profit in this move of 27 pips, you use a simple calculation: First multiply your total investment by the conversion for pips. If you invested $1,000 USD in the US currency, this is expressed as 1000 * .0001 = 1. Take this number and divide it by the currency trading rate of the currency pair: 1/1.1027 = .91. Now we take this number, representing the dollar per pip ratio of profit and multiply it by the number of pips .91 * 27 = 24.57. From this investment and a fluctuation of 27 pips, you have made $24.57, minus fees.

One additional note, while the pip generally refers to the fourth decimal place for all currencies, there is an exception with Asian currencies, where a pip is merely the second decimal place. For example one pip in regards to the Japanese Yen is reflected as 0.01. This is merely because of the way that the relative value of these currencies is stated. These currencies do not use decimal places, but rather have multiplied everything by one hundred to come up with relative prices. As such, think about 100 Yen as 1 USD; it makes sense pips are moved over two decimal places. Keep this in mind in regards to these Asian currencies, as it can be misleading unless you understand how pips are measured in these markets.

Stop-Loss Orders

Stop loss orders are a very helpful tool for traders, and even when not invoking the specific tool available from your broker, it is helpful to at least set up mental stop-losses for yourself. A stop-loss order is a lower bound for when you wish to pull out of a trade. You can issue to your broker an order saying that if a currency pair reaches a certain price, then you should sell all of your holdings. Stop-loss orders are exactly what they sound like, to stop you from losing any more money in the market. These orders are particularly helpful for value traders that are not monitoring their holdings constantly, and also for day traders that are working with many different currency pairs and have many different investments simultaneously.

Even when you don't set up an actual stop-loss order with your broker, you should set up a mental stop-loss. Find a price point where you no longer feel comfortable staying invested. Early on, this was a saving grace on trades that were not going well, but also when I wasn't sure if I wanted to stay committed. A huge part of being a successful trader is overcoming fear and staying true to your convictions. When real money is on the line, it is hard to determine the time in which you should pull out. A stop-loss order removes a lot of this stress because you are making a decision when your money is not at stake, allowing you to think through the risk in a reasonable way. The way in which I like to determine by maximum losses is percentage based. For example, if I make a $100 investment, the most I want to lose is twenty percent. I either have a mental stop loss order if I am monitoring the investment and it is a day trade, or I put in a physical stop-loss order with the broker if it is a value, or long term trade. Knowing your limits and using this feature from your broker will be essential in your early days and months of trading.

Currency Pairs

In chapter one you saw how money could be made from the exchange of currency and the passage of time. Specifically, you saw the transfer of US dollars to Euros and then back again. This is an example of a currency pair. When you buy into a currency, you are always buying into a specific currency pair. The base in which you pay for a pair is always in US dollars; so don't worry about where to get some of the first currency in a pair to buy the later, as US dollars are all that you will ever need. Currency pairs show a dynamic relationship between two countries, where the currency pair is reflective of the purchasing power of one country over another. In chapter one with the example of the Euro, European nations gained purchasing power over United States goods because of the decline in the US dollar's value. This is merely one example of how this dynamic relationship is useful to investors and businesses outside of strictly Forex markets.

Currency pairs are thought of as either standard pairs or exotic pairs, where exotic pairs fluctuate at a greater rate and/or have a relatively small volume. Exotic currency pairs are riskier to trade because with a smaller pool of investors, you lack the type of clarity in information that comes from trading larger currency pairs. Also, the small volume means that you may have difficulty offloading a currency at the time at that you want to. The reasons for the volume and volatility changes in exotic currency pairs are largely a function of one or both of the countries in a currency pair. The smaller the economy, the more volatile the currency is due to outside influence of the world – also the lower number of traders makes each trade more significant in changing the value. Examples of exotic currency pairs are: USD/DNK and USD/NOK. That is, the US dollar pegged against the Danish Kroner and Norwegian Kroner. While you may not think about Norway or Denmark as volatile countries, remember that is not what defines the exotic pair. Keep this in mind as you look at currency pairs, as it is not always obvious what is a standard pair versus exotic, although some brokers will actually label currency pairs as such.

Spread

If you are buying USD on a Forex market, you are not buying that currency directly from the US government. It is not being created out of thin air, but rather you are buying it from another trader. Understanding this, it makes sense that the trading value of a currency is rarely the actual value that you will obtain that currency for. The trading value is merely indicative of the average of the last few trades, or in some instances, the most recent trade. The people that you are buying currency from are traders like yourself, and they will want to make as much money as possible. To help buyers and sellers meet, we have the spread, which is the difference between the *ask* and *bid* price of a currency. For example, suppose that a currency pair is trading for 1.21, meaning you would gain 1.21 * the base currency's value in an exchange. You may only be able to find this currency trading at 1.2099, or a little higher or lower demanding on the demand. If the price that you are willing to pay is 1.21, but the best the seller can offer is 1.2099, we call the difference between these two numbers the spread. In this case, the spread is 0.001, or ten pips.

The reason why you need to keep the spread in mind is because it is a useful indictor for telling the direction that a currency is heading in. As the spread widens, it becomes more difficult to buy or sell a currency pair, as the spread narrows, the currency is highly liquid. An increase in spread usually means that a reversal is due, or at a minimum the currency value is going to slow down. You will want to use the spread to predict for future values, and also to gain insight for the best possible time to sell a currency. For standard currency pairs, volume will not be an issue, but for more exotic pairs the spread really starts to affect your ability to offload your holdings. How much the spread will be an influence on your ability to trade is therefore going to depend on the currency pairs that you are trading. As a beginner trader, you are best off starting with more established currency pairs so that you do not have to worry about volatility.

Candlestick

The candlestick is one of the most essential graphs for looking at the price history of a currency pair. A candlestick is a type of line graph that shows the fluctuation of price, where Y measures the price and X measures the time. What's unique is how each data point is represented:

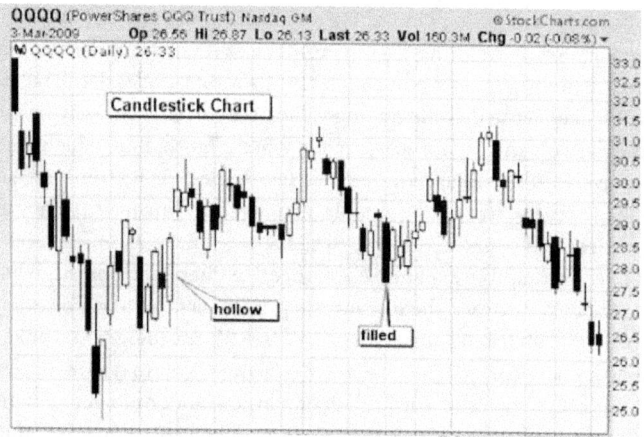

The above graph may seem quite confusing at first, but what is on display is a tremendous amount of information in the simplest way possible. Here we can see the simple X axis as time and the Y axis as price. The data points are made of candlesticks, where the filled in blocks represent declines in price, and the white hollow blocks represent an increase in price. This is at the heart of how candlesticks work, where by seeing this bit of information on each data point, you can see how each data point stands relative to all past data points. You can see that it is an increase or decrease at the flash of an eye, allowing you to measure a currency pair in different time intervals to different effect. Put simply, this graph could be presented on a yearly basis, daily basis, or over the last hour, where each data point could represent the month, day, hour, minute, etc. The candlesticks themselves are the individual unit of time in which we are measuring a currency pair. In addition to the candlesticks themselves, you will see a bar extruding from the top and bottom of the bar. This shows the magnitude of the change, where a tall bar at the top shows a positive change and a bar at the bottom shows a negative change. As for the length of the body of the bar, this shows the volatility in the currency's price, with longer blocks showing more volatility. If you invoke primarily analytical strategies this will be one of your main metrics, as you will thrive on volatility.

Reading a Currency Pair Graph

Remember that a currency pair is defined as a single ratio. As you are just getting started it can sometimes be difficult to identify how a currency pair ratio will affect the currency pair as a whole. For example, working with the NZD/USD pair, or New Zealand Dollar/US dollar pair, we can see the current exchange rate is 0.73. Imagine that you own US dollars and want to make a profit, in this scenario you would want this number to decrease. Looking at a graph this would be measured as a line with a negative slope. Please engrain in your head that as a line is going upwards, it is good if you are holding the first of a currency pair, if the lien is going downwards it is good if you are holding the second currency pair. I know this is a simple concept, but trust me when I say that a lot of people tend to read these graphs incorrectly. They are so accustomed to only wanting to see growth and a line chart go up, that they sometimes forget that is not in their best interest. I've seen this happen to smart people before – it is just a facet of this single ratio not always being intuitive for finding the positive direction for a single currency.

Options on Currencies

Don't trade options on currencies – this should be reserved for more advanced traders. That being said, some useful information can be gleamed from options markets for currencies. Very briefly, I want to explain the two types of options and what they mean. We have call options and put options, and each is the inverse of the other. With a call option, you are betting that a currency value will increase. With a put option, you are betting a currency value with decrease. If you see in the options market for currencies that there are a lot of calls on a currency, it means that a number of options traders believe that currency will increase in value. If you see a lot of put options, it is a signal that traders believe a currency value will drop.

Lastly, the way in which these options work is that they give the buyer of the option the choice to buy or sell currency for a certain price at a later date. In a call option, I'm betting a currency value will go up, so I pay a price for a contract that allows me to buy a currency pair for a lower price if the currency pair hits a certain price by a certain date. For example, if I am invested in the USD/EUR pair, and want the US Dollar to go up in value, then I pay for a contract that says I can buy USD at today's price if USD is trading at X by a certain date. If that date passes and USD has not reached that value, then the contract is worthless. If the price is met, then I can buy USD for a cheap price and sell it right away. Put options work in the opposite direction, where if I wanted USD to go down in value, I would pay for a contract that says USD will hit X price by a certain date. If USD goes down to that pre-arranged price then I can buy USD for a price set in the contract and then sell it right away. The contract will specify that I can buy it at a lower than currency market value, ensuring that I make money right away.

I wanted to give you a quick explanation of options because they are helpful for analyzing the market, but also to note where options traders make their money. Many options traders simply sell options, and they only make money when a contract does not go into effect. Keep this in mind, as this should be a powerful deterrent to starting with options. Traders early on will buy options based on the contract price, not realizing that even though the contract was well priced, the odds of the contract going into effect are astronomically low. Avoid options, but pay attention to what a number of call or put options on a particular currency pair mean.

Price Action

Price action is merely a term used to refer to how well or poorly a currency pair is trading. You can think about the price action as the 'swings' of a currency, whether that is positive or negative. In general, it merely describes a trending price movement in a currency pair.

Market Hours

One of the great things about Forex trading is that you will be able to trade day or night. There are markets that are open at all hours of the day. Look at the following list and you will see what exchanges are open and when. All the times listed are in standard Eastern Time, so adjust for your own time zone. Do note also that exchanges will sometimes sell the same currency pairs, and some exchanges will specifically sell other currency pairs. Also, the volume on these exchanges is not always the same from country to country. The New York exchange has greater volume than Sydney, for example.

New York: 8AM-5PM EST

Tokyo: 7PM-4AM EST

Sydney: 5PM – 2AM EST

London   3AM – 12PM EST

CHAPTER 4: ANALYTICAL APPROACH TO FOREX

Premise

I have two main methods of approaching Forex markets. I have found success in both strategies, but as you are just starting out and wrapping your head around the basics of the market, I suggest that you start with an analytical approach. What this means is that you are making trades purely based on existing trading data. You don't need to be tapped into the world of global politics, nor do you need to be aware of trade deals and agreements between companies across the world. You are merely looking at specific indictors and trading based on this data. This is a great trading method for beginners, and at upper tiers is great for statisticians or those that are apt at manipulating data. The best way to improve your analytical trading skills is to get better at using the various metrics for determining what currencies will rise, and which will fall.

Day Trading

Day trading is my primary strategy when it comes to Forex. This has been my bread and butter for two years, and although I have branched out in recent months, day trading has proven to be the main driver of my profits regardless of the climate in the markets. The premise to day trading is that you are holding onto currencies for a very short period of time, and are using cyclical data to predict ideal entry and exit points for a currency.

My typical day with this strategy starts by waking up two hours prior to whatever market I'm trading on. For example, I live on the east coast and typically trade on the New York exchange. I get up at six and start looking at currency pairs by around 6:30. I use the time before the market opens to identify currency pairs that have cyclical volatility, or rather have moved the last few days but have typically evened out by the end of the trading day. This is quite common to see in Forex markets, and there will be a general cycle to currencies, and in the long run they may lose or gain a few pips, but from a day-to-day approach they lose and gain value several times throughout the day. It is going to be through these small movements in a single trading day where I am going to make my money.

Once I have identified somewhere between three and five of these currency pairs, I plan my exit and entry points. You know that volume matters in terms of being able to sell off your holdings – if I am trading on exotic currency pairs that I pay strict attention to the volume of trading throughout the day, otherwise I can merely find the best price point to enter. When trading low volume currencies, you will need to pay closer attention to the spread to ensure that you are buying in and cashing out at the right times. Let's work with two quick examples.

In example one, I am going to buy a common currency pair, GBP/USD, or British Pound and the US dollar. I have decided to buy this currency pair because the price has been on a rotation for a few days, tending to hit max trading price at noon and going down again before the close of market. I decide that the time to buy is right as the market opens, because this is likely the time when it will be at the lowest price. I have also noticed that the stock is on a cycle of around 30 pips, meaning it moves about thirty pips each day. I decide that I will try and sell my holdings after around 30 pips of movement, and collect the profit for that day. This is a fairly straightforward example, and is the type of currency trading that you should focus on as you are just getting started. The type of tools needed to research this currency pair are fairly minimal, and looking at candlestick graphs for the last few days of trading would show this rotation in the currency pair's value. I have the leisure of waiting for around 30 pips of movement because this is a commonly held currency – I don't have to worry about my ability to offload my holdings. I would want to pay attention to the spreads to cash out when they are most in my favor, which in this case means narrow spreads.

For another trading example, let's work with a more exotic currency pair, USD/DNK. This is the US dollar trading against the Danish Kroner. In this example I am focusing on gaining value through this currency pair in a single trading day. The primary difference is going to be when I start to position myself for exiting the market. Suppose that this currency pair is trading at a cycle of 30-37 pips everyday for the last three days. I can therefore estimate that this currency pair will move this number of pips on the day that I take my position. I buy into this currency pair, hoping that the value of the Kroner will go up 30+ pips. Finding my entry point was a matter of finding the average lows for the last few days, assuming that the currency would not fall below that low on the day I take my position. Now here is the tricky part; we need to pay close attention t the spread for exotic currencies to be able to cash out at the ideal time. I'm expecting movement of 30 to 37 pips, but I'm actually going to start selling my holdings around 27-29 pips. Am I cutting into my potential profits? Absolutely, but it has happened to other traders and myself many times that if you wait for maximum profit on exotic currencies, the trading volume is so low that you end up cutting into your profits. Wait until over 3o pips and you are at tremendous risk. First of all, the price may not change by another 7 pips; it may start to decline at 30. Remember that this movement is merely an estimate, so we are looking at the lower bound and assuming this is when the price will hit its peak. As long as we start selling before the peak, we will make the most profit.

In short, day trading is a preferred style for many early Forex traders. The advantages are that research can be done outside of market hours (looking for the next day), and the tools that you need are not too advanced to be able to determine good picks for this strategy. If you start with two to four picks with a day trading strategy, you want to find success in around six to seven out of every ten trades. You are going to make very little profit on some of these trades, but this is where you will find improvement. It's simply a matter of being able to more accurately read graphs, but with day trading a standard candlestick for 24-72 hours, or even a line graph will be sufficient to find decent picks in the beginning.

Swing Trading

Swing trading has a lot of the same ideas as day trading, but the time scale is expanded to a few days instead of a single trading day. Fundamentally the strategy is the same as day trading. The main difference comes in how you use research tools to estimate the movement of a currency pair. There are two main techniques that I use to find currency pairs that are good for swing trading. Personally, I find this to be a little more research intensive than day trading.

The first technique is to focus on the immediate trading history of a currency pair. If you can find a currency pair with high volatility for one day, look into their past the last few days and see if you can start to identify a pattern. These cycles are not going to be as consistent in day trading, so the stretch from high to low is going to be more random. What you are looking for is merely the impression of a cycle; and build the parameters based on what you find. For example, suppose that you are interested in a relatively stable currency pair: GBP/USD, or British Pound to US Dollar. You see that there has been a lot of recent volatility and you start to look back a few days. You notice that yesterday, the pair moved -15 pips. The day before yesterday, the currency moved +10 pips. Three days ago the currency moved +12 pips. Four, five and six days ago the movement was: +7, -15 and -10, respectively. We may have found a good currency pair to get invested, but contrary to day trading, we want to buy our currency pair towards the end of the day, or when there is the least volatility. We may have a cycle of the currency moving for a few days in one direction, and then shifting in a second direction. We can use another tool to help us identify if this is a cycle, or some other occurrence maybe related to politics or volatility in the news. Checking the movement of the currency against the 25 day and 300 day high and lows for the currency pair, we can see that the currency pair is within its highs and lows for these two time periods. What this means is that it is increasingly likely that you have identified a cycle. Since the trading highs and lows are not outside of normal bounds, the pair is currently within well known territory, so we know that this is totally normal and expected behavior. Since the currency is not hitting new highs and lows, we can assume that within our cycle, we have a lower and higher bound for the cycle. We will want to buy in at the 25 day low, and then hold the currency until it has moved around 45 pips – this is based on the trading data for how far swings move for this pair.

The second technique is the functional opposite of the first. At first we were looking for currency pairs and making sure that their cycle is within the 25 and 300 day trading highs and lows. In the second technique we want to find currency pairs that are trading outside of either their 25 or 300 day highs or lows. It doesn't matter if they are trading above or below, just that they are different. In the first case, you find a currency pair trading below its 25 day high and low. From this, look past at the last few months to see how often it has climbed back from its lows. If it has consistently climbed back, buy into this currency pair. You will also want to look at the relationship of these countries and see if there is any recent news that is causing the price change in the currency pair. If there has been a news event, I would not trade on this currency. It is no longer predicable. If there is a no news or political cause for this price shit, you should get invested because there is bound to be a rebound based on the history of that pair's pricing.

In the second case, a currency is trading above its 300 day high. This is very unusual indeed, and might even call for shorting the currency through options, however you should only go down this path if you've been trading for a few months. The first thing you should do is look at the relationship between these two countries and any news that might have warped this relationship. You will almost certainly find that something has changed – you don't have breaks from 300 day highs or lows without some sort of event causing a shift in a currency pair's pricing. Based on this event, and the implications, you can start to buy in or short a currency pair. In this second case, it is very difficult to determine the amount of time that you should hold onto a currency. We are almost out of the realm of cycles, however we used analytical tools to find our position in this currency pair. We just confirmed or denied the relationship based on the news media from both countries. In the next chapter you will find that this is similar to a type of value trading, with the main difference how we came to find our picks. We based it on a change in the value of a currency based on the 300 day highs and lows, instead of jumping to the media to find a currency pair's relationship.

Scalping

Scalping is a top tier strategy. Like day and swing trading, you are still looking to identify cycles. The key here is that you are working on very, very small time intervals. I'm talking about buying a currency and holding it for less than an hour before selling it. This is a strategy that I strongly urge you do not focus on as you just start trading Forex. The key to developing a strong scalping method is to learn candlestick charts, and to gain insight into small cycles with your broker's toolset. For myself, I don't focus on scalping because the only way to make a really great profit is to take massive positions on a currency. For example, scalpers typically need to invest twenty to thirty thousand dollars to make a decent profit of a few hundred dollars. This simply isn't in the realm of many early traders. Even for myself I feel that the risk is not worth the reward in scalping. I merely wanted to include scalping in this section to inform you of this trading style, and also to look out for traders that have taken this approach to trading, as it will explain some of the rapid price movements or changes in spread – changes that cannot be explained with other trading strategies.

CHAPTER 5: VALUE TRADER APPROACH TO FOREX

Premise

Value traders take a very different approach to currency trading. While I focus on day trading, an analytical approach, I find that value trading is a great way to make longer term currency picks. These tend to individually pay off greater than day trading, but I find that they are altogether harder to find, limiting your number of active trades. The mentality of a value trader is that they are trying to find for market inconsistencies for a traded currency. Imagine the Chinese Yuan and how it is matched to the dollar. Ignoring that the Chinese Yuan is a harder currency to trade in general due to the heavy regulation from the Chinese government, the Yuan has a different issue in that it is currency not pegged to the right rate. This is not a secret – any economist and a handful of politicians will make the same claim. Relative to the US dollar, the Chinese Yuan is much stronger than its current trading value. For a value trader, they would buy as much Chinese Yuan as possible, and wait for the currency conversion to dollars be more favorable before they cash out. Now you can't actually do this with the Chinese Yuan due to some restrictions in how the currency is traded, but it serves the example that value traders are looking for currencies that are not pegged to the same rate. Finding currency that are traded free and fairly but are not traded on the correct rate is much harder to find than the Chinese Yuan, a well known manipulated currency.

Global Interdependence

Taking a value trader approach to Forex means that you need to be keyed in on how countries interact with each other. There is a strong relationship to the dollar and the Mexican Peso. For example, I know that if a number of car manufactures were to open plants in Mexico, the currency would experience a minor change change in favor of the Peso. This change will take months, if not years to be reflected in the currency price. Acting on this news I buy a stake in the Peso and wait for the currency to change. At the same time though, there are other elements that determine the trading value. A wall between Mexico and United States, or a change to the way that NAFTA (North American Free Trade Agreement) works, and suddenly my long term position might seem like a foolish investment. This is the risk and mechanics of this style of trading. You are trading based on news and information and your understanding of how countries interact. Profit is made when you are accounting for enough factors that will determine the price in the future. Mistakes are made when traders do not account for the proper variables.

Basic Strategies

Value traders tend to work in longer time frames than analytical traders, meaning they simply hold onto a currency for a longer amount of time. You should note that as a value trader you do not need to hold onto a currency for a long while to make a profit. During the 2016 US election, I was exchanging dollars and Pesos at a fairly rapid rate, only holding onto either currency in the pair for a few days. I was trading based on recent news events made popular by Donald Trump. He would go onto the campaign trail and start criticizing Mexico, or claiming that our trade deal was quite poor. When this would happen, the Peso would fall and the dollar would rise accordingly. I could have purchased dollars in this currency pair and made decent profit, but what was amazing was that the Peso always bounced back after Trump made a statement about Mexico. It was during this bounce back of the Peso that I made my profits. Some of these jumps were large, in the hundreds of pips. The time scale for investment in this scenario was only between one and three weeks. This is the type of value trading approach that I would suggest just as you get started in Forex. You don't want to trade on the complex interplay of countries based on long term relationships because odds are you do not understand every facet of those relationships. Instead, try a different approach and work based on news events and the immediate fallout that occurs.

2017 and On

I never thought the 2016 election would have lasting ramifications on the Forex market, but here I stand in 2017 with Donald J. Trump as the president of the United States. Never before has the trading market been so ripe for value traders to benefit off of the great instability that Donald Trump brings to the global economy. I have been working on theories to define the relationship that Donald Trump is going to bring to the global economy, and what I have found is not too far off what I discovered about Mexico. As a general rule when Donald Trump interacts with a country that is friendly to the United States, historically friendly as in helping in World War II, that currency gets strong for around a week. At the time that this book is being written, Trump has already made numerous statements and criticized many different countries. Most recently was a phone call between the United States and Australia. The AUD went up compared to the dollar because of this negative fallout from this phone call.

Here's how I would make trades in the future based on Donald Trump. When the United States and another country interact positively, the dollar goes up. If they interact poorly, the dollar goes down. Any statements made that affirm Russia as a global superpower or put NATO in jeopardy, and the Euro falls relative to the dollar. These have been the simple connections that I have found that have worked for my trades. I will continue to buy into currencies based on the impact of Trump, and I suggest you do the same.

CONCLUSION

Thank you again for downloading *Forex: The Basics You Need to Immediately Make Money from the Forex Market.*

You now have the skills necessary to start trading Forex and making immediate profit. Your first step to start trading is to choose a broker based on the currency pairs that you want to trade, the best rates, and the size of your investment fund. Refer to chapter two for a list of my preferred brokers. Next you will want to start with the analytical method of day trading to benefit from Forex. Note that this method has the advantage of you closing your balance books at the end of each day. In your first month of trading, it is good to know how well you have been doing on a day-by-day basis – a reason for sticking to this method as you first start trading. Remember that you will also want to start with standard currency pairs as you are trading, and hold off on exotic currency pairs until you've noted good trading volumes in currency pairs that you are interested in.

As you start trading and gaining experience, you will become better versed in how to manipulate trading data using your broker's tool set. It will take you around three months to truly get in the groove of making good day trading calls with high consistently. After you've reached this point, I suggest that you start making some value trades. These are trades that you are going to hold onto for a longer amount of time, but you are making these decisions based on news and the current geopolitical climate. Note that chapter five has a basic summary of some of the currency changes that you can expect in the future. If you can think through the interplay of countries, like how changing NAFTA will affect the CAD/USD pair, or the USD/MXN pair, then you will be in a position to earn tremendous profit.

As this book comes to a close, I want to stress the importance of building up your investment fund and never breaking from the ten percent rule. Always focus on building up your investment fund as a way of making larger trades, and never risk more than ten percent of your total fund. You have the tools to start trading, you have the knowledge, but you lack the experience – stick to this rule and you will be trading long enough to reap the benefits of this rule and the increased investment pool it brings.

Lastly if you enjoyed this book, it would be much appreciated if you could leave a review on Amazon. The best way for this book to make its way into the hands of more readers is through truthful reviews about this work. Please write what you liked about this book and what could be improved upon. Any and all feedback is helpful as I continue to serve the needs of my readership.

Thank you and good luck!